'*HERD* explained so much about why people really behave – things I'd always felt but now I had a soul-mate. *Copy Copy Copy* is a *must* must read – it's a brilliantly presented "how-to" guide for people who really want to change things.'
Mary Portas, Retail and Fashion Guru

'No one ever accused Motown of being unoriginal because it copied the production approach of Detroit's own Henry Ford. This delightful book argues magnificently that transferring ideas usually produces greater value than cooking them up from scratch. And then shows you how.'
Rory Sutherland, Vice Chairman, Ogilvy London and the *Spectator Magazine's* **Wikiman**

'Reasons to be Cheerful Part 3! Yet another entertaining handbook from the acclaimed Herdmeister for anyone involved in marketing, behavioural change and understanding why we all make the choices we make. Earls convincingly disrupts convention about what is innovation – through "praxis". This is jammed with great case studies and 52 actionable strategies. Shortly to be seen on a shelf near you.'
Stephen Maher, Chairman, The Marketing Society and CEO, MBA

'I have copied Mark a great many times in my career. I am looking forward to copying his new book with vigour, in the hope that one day he will copy me in return.'
Paul Graham, VP Creative Engagement, Burberry

'The book is the best thing written some corkers). It's also maybe the most useful and generous book about business or people I've read. It's a really important book (and it should be much more than a book to read once). You'll use it a lot.'
Gareth Kay, co-founder, Chapter San Francisco and former CSO, Goodby Berlin

'Finally! A rational case unpicking of our silly self-imposed obsession with always having an original idea. With a host of examples from Picasso and Matisse to Velcro, Elvis and The British Cycling Team and exercises and games to play to explore the ideas, Mark proves why copying often leads to good things as long as you ask the right "kinda" questions. *Copy Copy Copy* reaffirms why he is one of the great thinkers about social behaviour.'
Jamie Coomber, Global Head Digital Marketing, Converse

'Originality is a myth and it shackles creativity. Mark delightfully explains how copying is a fundamental aspect of being human and how copying and mutation is the foundation of all ideas. Both a rich intellectual dive into the nature of human behavior and ideas and a toolkit for you to pull from again and again, this is an invaluable and wonderful book. Get it and start copying because, after all, genius steals. I will for sure.'
Faris Yakob, co-founder, Genius Steals and author of *Paid Attention*

'*Copy Copy Copy* brilliantly marries the art of storytelling with tangible ways in which to take things that already exist and make them better! The examples and exercises detailed work just as well for the individual reader as for groups both large and small working with. This book is like no other, it is a highly engaging read which tackles some of the most significant challenges in business today with easy to use solutions.'
Julie Doleman, Managing Director, Consumer Division Experian Consumer Services

'In *Copy Copy Copy*, Mark Earls has once again worked his magic to distill the massively complex into the eminently simple. His thinking around how to explore problems and challenges is refreshing and his crystallization of the 52 strategic options is nothing short of genius. We've already used the ideas in our business and it really helped cut through the fog. I would recommend anyone to give it a try... It's a guaranteed cure for the curse of "strategist's block".'
Dominic Grounsell, Sales and Marketing Director, MORE TH>N, RSA Group and Chairman, Executive Committee ISBA

'I've long admired the new and original insights that Mark Earls has brought to the latest research into human behaviour and its relevance to brands and innovation. So frankly, I was disturbed to learn that his new book is in praise of copying. I need not have worried. Yet again this leading British business thinker has got us to see the world we inhabit today in fresh and mind-altering ways. His assessment of the impact of social media and its consequences are particularly pertinent to anyone dealing with the slippery business of brand strategy in the 21st century. It's also a book which marries theory and practice better than the vast majority out there. Most of all his message of copying one's way to greatness is entertaining, counter-intuitive and fun.'
David Abraham, CEO, Channel 4 PLC

'Oh joy, a book on marketing and behaviour change that's not only insightful, thought-provoking and fun to read, but can actually be applied too! For fans of Mark's earlier work – notably *HERD* and *I'll Have What's She's Having* – this is the book we've been waiting for; the next step on the journey from understanding how ideas spread to spreading your own ideas successfully. For anyone looking to make change happen, I recommend you get copying.'
Joe Jenkins, Director of Engagement, Friends of the Earth

Copy, paste, code, create, share. Tools long embraced by the creative world of the web. *Copy Copy Copy* is a brilliant guide to unlocking new forms of creative thinking for the modern world of marketing.'
Kathryn Parsons, co-founder and co-CEO, Decoded

COPY COPY COPY

How to do smarter marketing by using other people's ideas

Mark Earls

With illustrations by John V. Willshire

WILEY

This edition first published 2015
© 2015 John Wiley and Sons Ltd

Registered office

John Wiley and Sons Ltd, The Atrium, Southern Gate, Chichester, West Sussex, PO19 8SQ, United Kingdom

For details of our global editorial offices, for customer services and for information about how to apply for permission to reuse the copyright material in this book please see our website at www.wiley.com.

Wiley publishes in a variety of print and electronic formats and by print-on-demand. Some material included with standard print versions of this book may not be included in e-books or in print-on-demand. If this book refers to media such as a CD or DVD that is not included in the version you purchased, you may download this material at http://booksupport.wiley.com. For more information about Wiley products, visit www.wiley.com.

Designations used by companies to distinguish their products are often claimed as trademarks. All brand names and product names used in this book and on its cover are trade names, service marks, trademark or registered trademarks of their respective owners. The publisher and the book are not associated with any product or vendor mentioned in this book. None of the companies referenced within the book have endorsed the book.

Limit of Liability/Disclaimer of Warranty: While the publisher and author have used their best efforts in preparing this book, they make no representations or warranties with the respect to the accuracy or completeness of the contents of this book and specifically disclaim any implied warranties of merchantability or fitness for a particular purpose. It is sold on the understanding that the publisher is not engaged in rendering professional services and neither the publisher nor the author shall be liable for damages arising herefrom. If professional advice or other expert assistance is required, the services of a competent professional should be sought.

Library of Congress Cataloging-in-Publication Data

Earls, Mark.
  Copy, copy, copy : how to do smarter marketing by using other peoples ideas / Mark Earls.
     pages cm
  Includes bibliographical references and index.
  ISBN 978-1-118-96496-5 (pbk.)
  1. Marketing. 2. Consumer behavior. 3. Advertising. I. Title.
  HF5415.E24493 2014
  658.8'02—dc23   2014031895

A catalogue record for this book is available from the British Library.

ISBN 978-1-118-96496-5 (paperback)   ISBN 978-1-118-96498-9 (ebk)
ISBN 978-1-118-96497-2 (ebk)

Cover design: Parent Design Ltd.
Cover image credit: © Shutterstock/Eric Isselee
Page design by Andy Prior Design

Set in 10.5/16pt Sabon by Aptara, New Delhi, India
Printed in Great Britain by Bell & Bain

Note* on the typefaces used in this book

Sabon was 'created' in the 1960s for a group of German printers who wanted a "harmonized" font, i.e. one which would look the same, whether it was set by hand or on a Monotype or Linotype machine. However, it is not all that original, being clearly rooted in the successful fonts of the past – 16th Century styles like Garamond and Granjon, in particular. It looks better the larger you make it – which is why magazines like Vogue and Esquire use versions of it for headlines. For a long time, Sabon was Stanford University's official typeface.

Syntax is a humanist sans-serif face designed in the mid 1950s by the Swiss typographer Hans Eduard Meier. The story of its design is a classic one of copying creating error (see Chapter 2). Based on long-standing Roman lettering forms and inspired in particular by Morris Fuller Benton's New Gothic. The original sketches were done with a paintbrush, then the essential forms were captured by drawing the outline of the shapes created this way. Finally Meier added weights and variation to the resulting lettering to make it optically perfect in different contexts. And of course, he revised and adapted it over time as he learned more about how it reads.

*Sourced from Wikipedia…and the ageing brain of Grand Master Robbie Sparks

In Praise of Copying

Copying, originality, invention, innovation and the King of Rock 'n' Roll...1

How to Copy Well

Good, bad, tight, loose, close or far away 21

'What Kinda Thing?': Maps and Drawing

What kind of thing are you trying to change? 59

Where to Copy From: The Pattern Books

52 different strategies to copy, borrow or steal 89

Copy Better

Applying what we've learned to real world problems 129

CONTENTS

FOREWORD

by Walter Susini, Unilever

The way to get the originality we seek…might be through the simple – and very human – act of copying.

In marketing today, we place a much higher price on originality and creative excellence than ever before.

We love it.

We L O V E it.

When we have it, we want more.

When we don't, we scream and scream for it.

Because we know that this is one of the few remaining ways to create competitive advantage.

Which is why you're as likely to bump into a marketing person as an art director at the ad industry's get-togethers like the Cannes Festival. They want to know what the creative people do and how.

It's also why corporations pay people like me – poacher turned gamekeeper – to help them and their partners do better work.

And why 'derivative' or 'unoriginal' are one of the worst things you can say in modern marketing.

But we still don't know how to get 'original' ideas.

We don't always get the way the best new ideas and new strategies are created.

We'd like to pretend that it all happens in a deductive, predictable and repeatable way (like our manufacturing processes) but deep down, we know that it doesn't.

Equally we've long been told by those who define themselves as 'creative people' that there's something magical about having new ideas – that new things come out in a rush, a moment of inspiration, a rush of blood or a visitation from some muse or other.

But equally we know this isn't true, either. At least for most of the time.

So this book opens up a new and controversial possibility.

Because it shows us that the way to get the originality we want, isn't through straining and straining and praying and hoping for that shiny new thing to drop out of the sky.

But rather through the simple – and very human – act of copying.

In this book, Mark proposes that we learn to copy well (by which he means badly): loosely rather than tightly, from far away rather than from our immediate competitors.

Copying, he demonstrates, is paradoxically the best way to make things new and fresh and original.

If only you learn to copy well (badly, that is).

Not only does he give us the tools to copy well, a really simple set of questions to ask but a huge archive of things to copy (all neatly sorted into the types of behaviour we're trying to change or encourage).

I've long been a big fan of Mark's work – *Creative Age*, HERD and *I'll Have What She's Having*. They all changed the way I think about marketing, communication and how people really do what they do (as opposed to how we've been told they do).

Copy Copy Copy is different and more practical: it takes these ideas on and – enlightened by Mark's own experience – shows you how to put them to work.

Steal it.
Steal it all.
I know he'd want you to.

Walter Susini
GLOBAL VP CREATIVE STRATEGY CONTENT AND DESIGN

"If I have seen further, it is by standing on the shoulders of Giants."

— Isaac Newton, letter to Robert Hooke, February 1676

INTRODUCTION

On the Shoulders of Giants

OPTICS, MATHS AND THE SCIENTIFIC METHOD

Sir Isaac Newton was undoubtedly one of the most original and influential thinkers in the history of mankind. Without Newton, the modern world would be very different. Without Newton, there would be no Einstein, no Microsoft, no iPhone, no internet, no moonshot, no Facebook.

Newton invented the calculus that underpins modern mathematics and all that we do with it (as it turns out simultaneously with Gottfried Leibniz, even though Newton could never bring himself to concede the fact). His theory of light and optics transformed that field, too. His extraordinary synthesis of the work of Copernicus, Kepler and Galileo transformed the physical sciences fundamentally. So, for example, his laws of motion and gravity are still part and parcel of how we think about the physical world (Einstein and Heisenberg notwithstanding). Newton was without doubt the preeminent scientific mind of his day and was voted largely unopposed to the post

of President of the Royal Society (the leading scientific community of his day).

For all his talents and achievements he was not a nice man; not an easy person to love; not even very pleasant company. He was widely reported[1]:

> 'to have been an unsmiling and humorless, puritanical man with a countenance that was ordinarily melancholy and thoughtfull'.

Thomas Hearne, a precise contemporary, put it this way:

> 'Sir Isaac was a man of no very promising aspect. He was a short, well-set man. He was full of thought, and spoke very little in company so that his conversation was not agreeable.'

A grumpy little fellow, then.

For all his extraordinary gifts, it's hard to deny that Newton was a truly (brilliant?) terrible feuder, especially when it came to allocating ownership of ideas: for example, after the publication of the Principia, he had a series of bitter quarrels with his contemporary and sometime friend, Robert Hooke (the leading *experimental* scientist of the day and another irascible and difficult individual) over the latter's alleged contribution to Newton's work on gravity, motion and optics. Newton seems to have found it hard to give credit where it was due: the glory, in his mind, at least, was largely his.

This makes the letter to Hooke quoted at the start of the chapter all the more significant because it reveals how even Sir Isaac Newton was forced to acknowledge (even if only this once and in private correspondence) the role of others' work in his success. The full text runs thus:

'What Des-Cartes did was a good step. You have added much several ways, & especially in taking the colours of thin plates into philosophical consideration. If I have seen further it is by standing on the shoulders of Giants.'

On the shoulders of giants, indeed.

" Newton's work was built on the work of others. "

So even the greatest of physicists is compelled to admit that – far from being original and unique – his work was built on the work of others. He copied.

To be fair, this is the working method we know as the 'Scientific Method', used by Newton and his contemporaries in the 18th-Century Royal Society. This way of working creates a context in which scientists can stand on each other's shoulders – to use the work of others confidently.

However, it is not a case of merely assuming the truth of a fellow scientist's work based on status and reputation (which was how the 'natural philosophers' of the Middle Ages were forced to work). It is significant to note that the Latin motto of the Royal Society, *Nullius verba*, roughly translates as 'don't believe what they tell you just because they're important'.

The Method also discourages scientists adopting a view based on its plausibility (this is what *should* be or what we'd like to be the case). Instead, it insists on observable and verifiable fact: empirical evidence collected in a robust, transparent and reliable manner.

The method is not infallible by any means – even the practice of peer review can allow fashions and trends in ideas to spread, especially in the Social Sciences.[2] The

method can also be quite conservative in suppressing certain views that subsequently get accepted. Equally, new work can overthrow previously apparently well-grounded and long-held assumptions – for example Einstein's General Relativity exploits the fact that Newton failed to 'characterize' (describe in detail) what he means by Time and Space, 'these being commonly known', as the old man put it. Einstein merely took this lack of empirical foundation as a starting point for the work that was to challenge Newton's picture of the universe.

Newton, Einstein and all those scientists who have followed them; you, me and everyone who has ever lived: we build our kingdoms on the work of others, some we've met, some we'll never meet, some alive and some long dead.

" We all build our kingdoms on the work of others, often those we'll never meet. "

MARGINAL GAINS

Five years ago, few would have imagined that Britain would ever become the dominant force in competitive cycling – not France, not Italy, not Spain, not Germany, not the USA but Team GB – and do so both on the road and on the track.

In the first 98 years of the most famous road cycling event (the Tour de France), not one Britain appeared in the top three riders. Yet less than three years later, a British rider became overall champion and the British cycling team had managed to sweep seven out of ten gold medals at the Olympics. Cycling has now become a mainstream sport in this country – both on the road and on the track; for spectators and for athletes.

The story of how they did it starts and ends with one man and his determination to learn from elsewhere.

When Dave Brailsford took over as Team Sky performance coach, he and the team leadership set very clear goals for themselves and developed a very simple strategy (which Brailsford himself has credited to his MBA studies at Sheffield Hallam University): 'the aggregation of marginal gains'. Put simply, this is a version of 'look after the pennies and the pounds will look after themselves' – focus on creating a host of very small advantages which together add up to a big one. First at Team Sky and then at the British Olympic cycling team.

Brailsford has often revealed his debt to Billy Beane (the legendary Oakland A's baseball coach, immortalized in *Moneyball* by Michael Lewis):

> 'to have someone come in and say: "Are we measuring the right things?" was refreshing … Beane stood back and said he wasn't going to go with conventional wisdom … it's refreshing that there was an industry where everyone thought in one way until a guy came along and said "hang on a minute".'[3]

Brailsford's use of statistics has helped him make better decisions about team selections and when to invest in particular players, as well as when to axe them. He is part of a group of elite performance 'statties' working in UK elite sport (like Mike Forde at Chelsea FC and Damien Comolli of Liverpool FC) who learn from each other and across sporting boundaries.

In cycling, this kind of numerate mind-set allowed the Olympic team to calculate exactly how much further

they would need to travel how many more turns of the wheel – and how much time they would lose, if the riders strayed more than 4 cm from the black race line: in these small margins victories and defeats are built. As Al Pacino says in *Any Given Sunday*:

> 'You find out life's this game of inches. And so is football … The inches we need are everywhere around us.'

Brailsford brought in expertise and techniques from a host of distant disciplines (rather than from other cycling coaches): from epidemiology, from sleep science, from nutrition, from any other field that seemed capable of giving his athletes a marginal advantage. He has talked at length about team building with the manager of the most successful soccer club in the world, Manchester United's Sir Alex Ferguson, while also fretting about how to use medically approved hand-washing techniques to reduce the incidence and spread of viruses and bugs, which can impact the riders' ability to perform.

> 'Do you really know how to clean your hands? Without leaving the bits between your fingers?[4]

" Copying wins cycle races. "

Brailsford's 'aggregation of marginal gains' is an incredibly powerful overall strategy but it depends on learning from – *copying* – the specialist expertise that studies those margins. Copying wins cycle races.

HIS DARK MATERIALS

Phillip Pulman is one of the most successful novelists of the modern era: his *Dark Materials* trilogy has sold more than 20 million copies, won prize after prize from the critics and stolen the hearts and minds of readers around the world with its complex and subtle fantasies of parallel worlds, science, faith, impending disaster and make-or-break moral choices facing the young and the powerless. As the late Christopher Hitchens puts it, Pullman has performed the apparently impossible feat of 'dissolve[ing] the frontier between adult and juvenile fiction' – remarkable for any author, for this or any other era, but honed, we suspect by 20 years of sharing his enthusiasm for the great Greek myths with high school students.

Perhaps Pullman's most memorable invention is the narrative device of the 'daemon' – a visible and tangible animal-shaped soul that his *Dark Materials* characters can't help but display to each other. As a story-telling device, the 'daemon' allows Pullman all kinds of interesting narrative opportunities – subtly suggesting elements of an individual character's personality that they'd rather keep hidden or dramatizing the psychological impact on an individual's psyche of interacting with other, more forceful characters.

So when an interviewer asked recently[5] about Pullman's own 'daemon', he revealed that:

> 'she's a bird of the crow family ... scruffy old thing! She steals things – anything bright and shiny.'

Which explains the source of his own literary invention:

> 'I steal story ideas. I'm quite happy to steal them from Shakespeare or from soaps on TV (funnily I steal a lot from Neighbours) ... or from the top of the bus.'

" Copying lies at the heart of creativity. "

Copying – for Pullman at least – lies at the heart of creativity.

As it turns out, he's not alone in thinking this.

TALENT COPIES

Picasso had a very similar perspective about the central role of copying in art and artists' attempts to make art: 'talent copies, genius steals' he famously observed (as my old chum, Faris Yakob, reminds us all.

TS Eliot went further, suggesting that while all poets copy by necessity, bad ones merely 'deface what they copy; great ones make something better or at least different'.

Famously William Shakespeare, the greatest writer in the English language filched his plot lines from the manuscripts he found on the bookstalls of the City of London (only three of his plots are original in the sense that he created them without a primary external source). However, he used that copying to create new and different versions of the storylines he'd filched.

❝ Only 3 of Shakespeare's plots are original. ❞

George RR Martin, author of the books which have become the smash hit TV series *Game of Thrones*, recently confessed to the same approach:

'In A Song of Ice and Fire, I take stuff from the Wars of the Roses and other fantasy things, and all these things work around in my head and somehow they jell into what I hope is uniquely my own.'[6]

Finally Voltaire – the great French intellectual action hero of the Enlightenment and champion of independent rational thought (as opposed to received wisdom) – described creativity in a somewhat downbeat way, as nothing more than 'judicious imitation'.

So let's consider the case of one Elvis Aaron Presley, 17-year-old truck driver, only son of a white trash couple in Memphis, Tennessee. How do you think he managed to get to climb to the top of the cultural tree – to become, as the composer and conductor Leonard Bernstein put it, 'the greatest cultural force in the twentieth century. He introduced the beat to everything, music, language, clothes, it's a whole new social revolution—the 60s comes from it'?

Did he achieve this through pure originality – by working things out all on his own? By squeezing the music until something original and world-shaking emerged? Or, by taking the music and the style and the dance of those he saw around him on Beale Street and creating his own version.

Elvis was the King of Rock 'n' Roll but he was – as we shall see – also a big fat copycat.

WHY DOES ANY OF THIS MATTER?

All of us are struggling to innovate – to find new solutions to old problems, to find new ways of working, new ways of thinking that might just – please, Lord, this time – work better than the old ways; that work faster, more sustainably or just more efficiently. We strive to find new products and new strategies to keep up with the rapidly changing outside world (and the demands of our competition and our financial overlords).

Of course, some of this is driven by a neophilia – an insatiable desire for the new, whatever the cost and whatever the value, one of the hallmarks of our contemporary culture – but much of it is better-intentioned than that.

> ❝ **We all want new answers and new solutions for the very real and very pressing challenges that our organizations face.** ❞

We all want new answers and new solutions for the very real and very pressing challenges that our organizations face. We want new things to point to and talk about: new ideas and new policies.

Now we've learned an awful lot in recent years, specifically from the software and service industries about how we organize our work – about being more 'agile' and prototyping rapidly. All of which helps the speed we get to market and our ability to learn from customers (even if it ignores the absolutely central role of copying in the day-to-day business of writing software) – without cut-and-paste, each and every line of code has to be written afresh. Far better and easier to reuse other coders' work e.g. via code directories and similar.

IF IT WASN'T FOR YOU PESKY KIDS

All kinds of organizations struggle with challenges that involve humans, such as in the domains of marketing, behaviour change and change management. Doing anything with this human element is naturally messy, confusing and in many ways unpredictable. Human behaviour is a complex phenomenon and genuinely hard to change (think of how hard it is to change the behaviour of those closest to you and then think again about people you haven't met and scale this up by hundreds, thousands and then tens of thousands).

> ❝ **Human behaviour is a complex phenomenon and genuinely hard to change.** ❞

Whatever the folks that run behaviour change programmes tell you, these are always much less successful than you'd imagine – most such programmes inside organizations go the way of all the rest, leaving some odd marks on the company organogram and a few quirky t-shirts and coffee mugs. This is part of the reason why resorting to M&A to drive growth is almost always a bad bet – getting two groups of people feeling anxious for their jobs to do the one thing is more than twice as hard as getting one group to do so.

Equivalent programmes outside the organization generally fare no better – even at its best, marketing is a weak rather than a strong force in business (which is why we celebrate successes when we see them) and most governments' attempts to change the behaviour of their citizens are far less successful than anyone would like to imagine, certainly not as effective as the minister announcing the programmes seems to believe (which is why the appropriately named Behavioural Insights Team at the UK Cabinet Office represents such a step forward in policy design).

So it's worth asking yourself: why do you persist in the search for your salvation in the new – the brilliant and novel solution that you haven't yet found – when you can more easily copy something that's worked before?

THE TYRANNY OF THE SINGULAR

Part of the reason why we do is that we like to treat each such problem or challenge as unique – as unlike anything that we have faced before – one which demands a unique and singular solution. This is what I call the *tyranny of the singular*.

> " **Part of the reason why we do is that we like to treat each such problem or challenge as unique.** "

A unique problem is flattering to both problem owner and would-be solver (one is elevated in status by the unique nature of the challenge in front of them – yes, it is genuinely tricky to sort out and only the best is up to this kind of thing – and the other by the unique skills and strategic genius/magic it must take to solve it).

But this attitude is genuinely unhelpful to both parties: it can make it seem nigh on impossible to solve any one given problem, except through superpowers, derring-do and so on. We recently worked with a client who unintentionally hindered their people from solving the central strategic challenge facing the organization by describing it as being 'like changing the tyres on an F1 race-car, doing 250 mph

BUT without slowing down or entering the pit lane'. That is, impossible without a magic wand or TARDIS, or both.

Seeing things as singular is genuinely flattering to both problem owner and would-be solver. But equally unhelpful.

Equally our expectations of the unique and special nature of the appropriate solution – the prince come to rescue us from the tower – often leads us to dismiss perfectly acceptable and workable solutions on the basis of their familiarity and effectiveness elsewhere (the very basis on which we should be considering them). In other words, the tyranny of the singular makes it harder to select or buy good solutions, too.

Why not copy something that has worked elsewhere?

NOT ALL COPYING IS GOOD

Before we go any further it is worth acknowledging that this kind of talk makes many people feel uncomfortable. And not just because of assumptions about the singularity of each problem and the requisite heroic qualities of those who can tackle these singular challenges.

No, many of us also feel uncomfortable because our individualist culture which so values originality, disdains and stigmatizes copying.

> ❝ **Our individualist culture values originality and disdains and stigmatizes copying.** ❞

Consider how hard our culture works for this individualism: we are encouraged to 'self-actualize' (literally the ultimate need-state according Maslow and co.), to find our own song, our own lifestyle and our own selves, either on the therapist's couch, in the dark self-help aisle of the bookstore or on some long, dark night of the soul.

This, we are taught, is where original ideas and things come from – the lone (sometimes tortured) genius working their magic in splendid isolation. We look to our individualist innovative heroes – Picasso, Shakespeare, Newton, Jobs, Freud, and (and their heroic journeys to create their work and earn the public's appreciation – even if the latter only comes posthumously after a life of struggling poverty, general rejection and single-minded isolated creativity). By contrast, it is copying that we hold responsible for all that is mediocre and worthless, in art as in commerce. As Oscar Wilde puts it, 'most people are other people: their thoughts someone else's opinions, their lives a mimicry, their passions a quotation'.

By contrast, we imagine that the crowd – The HERD – could not possibly create anything. Hence the long standing use of the black sheep motif by the great creative agency, BBH to highlight the renegade and anti-ovine nature of their creativity. And equally, by way of counterblast, my use of the Warhol-ish sheep in the design of this book.

My point is here is simple: original ideas, things and strategies are the product of many hands (and brains) and not of the one-man band. It's what we learn from each other – what we copy – that allows us to create new things. Copying can – in the right circumstances – and does create novel and effective solutions to problems. Copiers can and do produce novelty and value far more than the solo act (in fact, as we've seen, the greats have always – well nearly always – seen copying as a central drive of their working practice). As the political journalist Owen Jones puts it:

> We are socially constructed beings, forming an immense dynamic system that cannot be understood by reducing it to its individual parts…The good or bad that we do has the fingerprints of others all over it."[7]

But that's not how it feels, right? When you realise that George Harrison's *My Sweet Lord* is effectively (albeit unconsciously, according to the NYC circuit judge's ruling) the same song as Jimmy Mack's *He's so Fine* (a hit for the Chiffons, back in the day), it's hard not to feel worse about the ex-Beatle's tune. Copies are never as good as originals, right?

Let's be clear: not all copying is good; indeed, copying that aims for replication, mimicry or the practice that business calls 'benchmarking' – all styles of 'tight' copying AKA '*single white female*' copying (after the movie of the same name - see Chapter 2) often reduce value rather than increase it.

'Tight' or SWF copying can often be as bad a strategy than *not copying*.

" Copying with a twist or copying from further away – is what the world needs more of. "

By contrast, 'looser copying' – copying with a twist or copying from further away – is what we think the world needs more of. We'll explore lots of different ways to do this, later in the book.

So in order to really embrace copying, you're going to have to do more than learn how to do it well (or badly); first, you're also going to need to overcome the cultural stigma around copying and copiers.

WHY COPYING MATTERS

This is what I'm arguing for here:

- Copying is a great hack for developing new people strategies. ('hack' as in short-cut or fast-track, not 'hack' as in phone-hack).
- Copying is not difficult to do. It remains one of the great human gifts – forget 'monkey see, monkey do'. Humans copy earlier, better and longer than our simian cousins.
- Copying means you don't have to think every problem through on your own: you get to do more than 'phone a friend'. You get to use the brains, experience and success of others as much as you like: others you've never met and sometimes others long dead. You're not left facing the beast, armed only with the thoughts that you can have yourself – it's like having an army behind you or the entire *X-Men* crew at your shoulder.
- Copying also means you don't have to see every problem in isolation – as a unique and never-seen-before freak of nature. You can start to see different types and classes of problems and learn from each.
- Copying also means you can get to go faster – using other people's successful strategies enables you to be 'agile' (as the current fashion has it): to spend less time doing what the strategic planning guru, Henry Mintzberg, calls 'Strategy as Planning' and more time *doing* strategy.

For the reasons just discussed, everywhere you look strategy thinking expands to fill the time available and then some. Copying means you don't have to do all the thinking as a priori thinking – it gets you to do more thinking-as-doing (and thus learning and adapting and evolving your people strategies in response to the market rather than wait until they are all shiny and perfect …). As Facebook's walls shout, *done is better than perfect*.

Copying fills the space at the beginning of any agile process concerning humans – it helps you make sure that you've got effective content to work with through that process.

MORE THAN A MASH-UP

However, this is more than a general discourse on the virtues of copying. In recent years we've all observed and discussed remix culture and 'mash-ups' and so on. Some of us have developed an abiding love of hip-hop culture (even though we're not from South LA) and street art (various), which we like to display in our nice middle-class apartments.

No, this book proposes a fundamental rethink of how you go about solving problems – of how you should go about developing strategies to solve these tricky human-shaped challenges that we face inside and outside every organization.

By copying.

AFTER THE HERD

My previous two books, *HERD* and *I'll Have What She's Having* (the latter with Professors Alex Bentley and Mike O'Brien), both stopped short of providing specific recommendations about what to do with the map of how people do what they do that I was trying to describe.

I was happy describing a better map to help readers better navigate the kinds of human-based challenges discussed already. I felt it was enough merely to stimulate our peers and contemporaries to work out new answers to the question of how to change behaviour for themselves.

Since then, I've had many interesting conversations with readers of all sorts, in marketing and the military,

For those who haven't read those two (highly recommended) tomes, the first essentially argues that many aspects of human behaviour that we take to be rooted in what goes on between an individual's ears are in fact shaped by what goes on between that individual and their peers – the HERD; the second lays out a simple data-led map to think about different kinds of me-behaviour and we-behaviour, harnessing the latest social science to illustrate the nature of that map and the categories it creates.

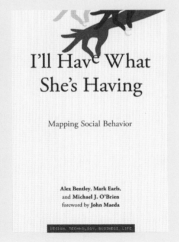

in politics and the c-suite, many of which have opened my eyes to new applications of the map but all of which have made it clear that we need to go further, to provide more practical guidance. As Marx observed: 'The philosophers have only interpreted the world, in various ways; the point is to change it.'[8]

So this book is – to use the jargon – as much about *praxis* as it is about *theory*, about doing rather than describing. About how and what you should copy as much as about why you should copy and copying's interesting history.

About how to use your 'sheep-inside'.

DIFFERENT KINDS OF QUESTIONS

At the heart of the new approach I describe in the following pages are some very different kinds of questions to the ones most strategists ask:

What kind of thing is this? What is it like?
What kinds of solutions have worked elsewhere and for similar kinds of things?
What is our version?

These 'kinda' questions break open the singularity trap and help you access the appropriate examples to try out in the real world.

But you also need to know what to copy – what kind of thing works to solve similar kinds of problem. You could just go for some of what you fancy – the strategies your favourite brands adopt or your favourite marketer or business guru recommends. Much of the time this will be better than sweating the singularity.

But even better would be to use our archive of 52 different kinds of successful strategy, sorted by 'kinda' thing – by behaviour type – so that you can very quickly go from 'kinda' thing to 'kinda' strategy, to example and then on to prototype. And then start to learn what seems to work and what doesn't for the challenge you are faced with.

THE AMBITION OF THIS BOOK

That's why I've developed this book in five chapters with a mix of ideas and practical things to do.

1 In Praise of Copying: an exploration of our rather odd ideas about copying, originality and creativity and copying's surprisingly central role in shaping human behaviour and advancement. This is a clearing of the ground for the work proper.

2 How To Copy: copying well and badly, tightly and loosely, asking 'what kinda thing?' questions.

3 What Kinda Thing: this chapter helps you get familiar with our 'kinda' sorting box, which will help you work out where to copy from.

4 Where to Copy From: the archive of more than 50 different kinds of strategy appropriate for different kinds of problem.

5 Copy Better: more examples from my own practice and from those of colleagues and peers. By applying yourself and the ideas and strategies to these challenges and creating your own 'versions', I hope to give you the confidence to do so for yourself.

Overall, I want to encourage more use of copying in marketing, in management, in policymaking and in behaviour change in the broadest sense. I want to help you learn to copy more often and to copy better (by which we mean *worse* – more loosely, from further away and to copy more than one solution). And I want you to feel good about doing so.

COPIED FROM PEOPLE WHO'VE COPIED

A lot of this work arises from the collaboration that I've been fortunate enough to develop over the last seven or so years with Professor Alex Bentley of Bristol University. Specifically his extraordinary knowledge of the behavioural science literature, his intellectual generosity and his incredible practical expertise have helped to create, for example, the 'kinda' sorting box and to develop this way of solving problems together.

At the same time, I've been fortunate enough to do a lot of work with John V. Willshire of Smithery (the inventor of the Artefact Cards and the illustrative style, which you will see popping up throughout the book). His contribution to the thinking and the practice here is immeasurable (literally so) – not least in his detailed reading of the text.

But that's not a full and complete list of collaborators – some of the people I respect most have added – whether knowingly or not – to this thinking (see Acknowledgements).

I've tried to capture the flavour of our work in the way I've put this book together – informed but useful, serious but playful at the same time. For example, at the beginning of each chapter I summarize what the chapter contains: I've also included suggestions of games you might play and things to do – puzzles to solve and ways of thinking through issues, as well as some texts you might

want to consult for further exploration of the ideas we borrow here.

LEARN TO CODE OR LEARN TO COPY?

There's a lot of noise in business today about the importance of learning to code (to write software code) and there's a lot to be said for doing so (I enjoyed greatly my day with Richard and Kathryn from Decoded and would recommend this kind of thing wholeheartedly).

However, in my view, learning to *copy well* (or, as it turns out, copy *badly*) really should be one of the central parts of any business education. Whether you work inside or outside organizations or in the space between them and their customers or other stakeholders, whether you work in marketing, in policy or in general management, learning to copy well should be mandatory.

And if you need any greater encouragement, it's always worth remembering, as the stories at the beginning of this introduction demonstrate, copying just happens to be the go-to tool of the great innovators and is part and parcel of making great creative work. It's entirely natural (it's one of our great gifts as a species) and makes great stuff – what more could you ask for, honestly?

If it's good enough for Elvis, Newton, Pullman, Braisfield, Shakespeare and Picasso, *isn't it good enough for you?*

> **Most people are other people: their thoughts someone else's opinions, their lives a mimicry, their passions a quotation.**
>
> —Oscar Wilde

What this chapter will cover:

This chapter explores the conflicting and conflicted ideas we have about originality and copying, deception, fakery and identity.

There are few things we like more than originality and few we dislike more than copying. The rights and wrongs seem clear-cut and unarguable.

However, it turns out that our discomfort with copying is not shared by the rest of humanity – it's a peculiarly Anglo-Saxon and very recent phenomenon.

Equally contemporary science shows how important copying is to all of us – as individuals, as societies and as a species.

In particular, copying lies at the heart of innovation – no copy, no innovation.

So what better place to start than with that 'unique artist – an original in an area of imitators', Mr Elvis Presley?

Uh-huh!

1 IN PRAISE OF COPYING

Copying, originality,
invention, innovation
and the King of
Rock 'n' Roll

WELCOME TO ELVISLAND

Few events on the planet capture our mixed-up and confused feelings about copying better than the annual Elvies festival, held each October in an unprepossessing purpose-built holiday resort outside the seaside town of Porthcawl in wet and windy south Wales. The Elvies is the world's largest such gathering devoted to His Presleyness (it has a daily attendance only slightly lower than the much cooler and well-funded Burning Man Festival). Over the course of one autumnal weekend, out where the brown-grey waves of the Bristol Channel meet the post-industrial landscape of the Welsh coast, more than 100 acts strut their stuff – shake their hips and curl their lips – and present their impersonations of the one and only – The King.

In 2012 the Elvies achieved something particularly special: it witnessed the largest ever recorded gathering of Elvis impersonators doing their snake-hipped best, rather rowdily singing along to 'Hound Dog' (smashing the record held by a Nike US sales conference some two years previously).

Elvies organizer Peter Phillips noted, 'We had all sorts of different Elvises aged from three to 80 and from the UK, Ireland, Germany, Malta and even Brazil. They were wearing all manner of Elvis costumes from gold lamé jackets, to leather jump suits and GI uniforms.'[9] (Although, if the photographic evidence is anything to go by, the predominance of rather paunchy Vegas Elvises says something about the festival's demographic.)

1-2-3-4: off they go – jumping, gyrating, shaking, uh-huh-ing and vairmuch-ing.[10]

COPYCATTING AN ORIGINAL

On the surface, the Elvies is a celebration of copying – of impersonations of the great man whom we all acknowledge as one of the great innovators. The man Mick Jagger dubbed 'a unique artist – an original in an area of imitators'.

❝ The Elvies is a celebration of copying. ❞

As with most Elvis-related events, the majority of people seem happy with the kind of mimicry on show – no-one is actually seriously pretending to be Elvis even if they've got his moves down to a 't'. Nobody's deluding themselves or anyone else – apart from the 'guy [who] works down the chipshop [who] swears he's Elvis', as the song has it.

Some of the Elvises of course are more Elvis-y than others: some have more of the voice, some have more of the looks or the costume or the legs. And for those that don't really have any of these things, the weakness of their impersonation is taken in good spirit. Good and bad copying seem to be equally well-received: accurate and inaccurate turns alike. Fat Elvis or thin Elvis, young (and there are some very young Elvises – young enough to be great grandchildren of his Uh-Huhness) or old Elvis. Every Elvis is good in Elvisland.

Even if that great Welsh Elvis-a-like, Michael 'Shaky' Barrett (AKA 'Shaking Stevens') – were to stumble in and run through any one of his 33 (!) UK Top 40 Elvis-style singles, still we'd all be happy: while he still appears and moves like Truck Driver Elvis, we know and he knows and we know he knows his copying is not meant as a bad thing but as an 'homage' or something similar.

But beyond all this happy copying of different degrees of faithfulness, on another level, nobody seems to want to mention the fact that the object of all this copying – the Original, the King himself – wasn't perhaps quite as, well … *original* as all that.

" The King himself – wasn't perhaps as original as all that. "

ELVIS-A-LIKE

Let's start with his handle – the Elvis name is no one-off, no 'moonunit' neologism (the name Frank Zappa famously gave his son).

Indeed, the name Elvis has a long and honourable past: it is an anglicized version of the name of a real 6th-Century Celtic bishop, Saint Ailbe (alternative spellings include Ailbhe, Elfeis, Ailfyw, Ailvyw, Elveis, Albeus), who supposedly baptized the patron saint of Wales, St David. The abandoned ruins of the church of St Elvis don't sit outside Memphis, Tennessee, nor just off the strip in Vegas, but in a farm on the cold wet hillside about 4 miles east of the city which bears the name of Wales' Patron Saint, looking out towards Ireland, where *that* Elvis lived. His mother's name is undeniably Welsh (Gladys); his surname too seems to be of local origin: the North Pembrokeshire *Preseli* (sic) Hills run some 13 miles from Dinas Island to Crymych through what is now the Pembrokeshire Coast National Park. Although, as is so often the case, the geographical origins of the family's name are not something

that the owners are aware of – a name is just a name after all, even if it is handed down over many generations.

Elvis was and remains a covers artist.

Nor was the music Elvis made all that new: it was a mix of the stew of RnB and Blues and Gospel and such like he heard near Memphis' Beale Street where he had his first (truck driving) job; the songs all covers, not originals, including tracks from The King's early Sun Sessions like *That's All Right, Mama* by Arthur 'Big Boy' Crudup and *Blue Moon of Kentucky*, a 1947 hit for Bill Monroe and his Bluegrass boys. While in later years, his management attempted to secure co-writing credits for the songs the man recorded, Elvis was and remains a covers artist – not some auteur, singer-song-writer or inventor, singing the songs of his heart and his own creation but someone who sang the songs of someone else. As any amateur musician will tell you, there's a world of difference between the status of those who 'write their own material' and 'covers bands'.

'Real' musicians, we imagine, create their own music, write their own tunes and their own lyrics; by contrast we consider 'cover' artists as musical freeloaders – not talented enough to do their own thing. It's worth noting that this is both a passing idea (for much of the history of the music industry, it has been as much if not more the performance of a song that matters – the product of the interpreter's rather than the songwriter's efforts and skills') and one dependent on the cultural context

(the notion of the 'auteur' performer and the singer songwriter flourished particularly in the latter part of the 20th Century).

Of course, there are cover artists and then there are cover artists – the local wedding band are not a patch on Elvis, surely? Even my band, the Mighty Big Shorts, are a covers band. It makes us feel slightly better – when faced with the disdain of proper muso's moonlighting as sound-engineers – to recall that The King often sang other people's songs better than the composers could do so themselves (even if the same cannot strictly be said of our shows).

Even Elvis' famously shocking cover of Hound Dog was stolen from a local band.

But even Presley's iconic covers of other people's tunes were often not his own: his version a copy of other's covers. His rendition of *Hound Dog* is seen by many as his breakthrough number but it was not fresh out of the box – the Leiber and Stoller song had already been a genre hit for blues singer Willie Mae 'Big Mama' Thornton. Thornton's version created such a splash that it spawned a handful of country-style covers and a bizarre selection of 'response' and spoof records (including 'Bearcat' with re-written lyrics by Sun's own Sam Phillips).

Elvis' shocking, highly sexualized version made him a national phenomenon when he played the Milton Berle

Show in NBC-TV on 5 June 1956. While the first 90 seconds of the tune were performed uptempo, the final minute was what got the nation's parents uptight:

> 'slowing the pace, Elvis bent the mike toward him and performed a series of slow pelvic thrusts… the sexual symbolism was all too obvious'[11]

But this, too, was copied from a local band, Freddie Bell and the Bellboys, whom Elvis and his band saw in Vegas. 'When we heard them perform that night, we thought the song would be a good one for us to do as comic relief when we were on stage. We loved the way they did it', noted guitarist Scotty Moore. So what did they do? They copied it.

You could say that the distinctive sound that Elvis brought out of the original Sun Sessions in July 1954 was the product of an accident rather than a deliberate 'invention' too: when Elvis, Scotty Moore and Bill Black were playing around with *That's All Right, Mama*, playing it at double speed and so on, producer Sam Phillips stopped them and asked, 'What are you doing?' 'We don't know', they said. Phillips had found the sound he was looking for. 'Back up and do it again', came the voice from the control room.[12] Copy, copy, copy.

SHAKE A LEG

Even Elvis' distinctive stage outfits were not novel creations. They were chosen off the shelf (or peg) for him by someone else. Beale Street tailor Bernard Lansky served those with a taste for flash and a 'real sharp look' – 'musicians, gamblers and hustlers from across the Mississippi delta'. The teenage Presley spent a lot of time around Beale Street, absorbing both the music and the style, and window-shopping at Lansky's. Lansky was fond of describing their first meeting: 'He [Elvis] said, "When I get rich, I'm going to buy you out." I said, "Don't buy me out. Just buy from me." And he never forgot me.'[13]

Elvis' look throughout his career was shaped by Lansky's interpretation of the style of Memphis hoodlums of the times – from the peg-trousers and two-tone shoes of the Sun Studios era to the jumpsuits of later years, including the white suit and blue tie in which Elvis was buried. 'I put his first suit on him and his last suit on him' Lansky said.

And yet to most of us, Elvis remains The Original, The King, The One and Only.

His looks, his interpretations and his performances and the story of his sad, lonely death unique and unrepeatable (except by all those Elvis impersonators). Elvis remains both original and copy.

" Elvis remains both original and copy. "

Original and copy: two things that don't go together. Like Superman and Kryptonite. Or oil and water. Or so you might like to think.

COPYING IS CHEATING

There are few things our culture esteems more than novelty and originality; few it despises more than copying.

On the one hand, we love new things, new ideas, new solutions, new news, original and authentic things. Let's have some new ideas, rather than revisit the old ones. Politicians need to have new answers not (unless they are of a particular nostalgic bent or unaware of their own thinking) recycle old ones. This is why politics in the developed world is awash with 'thinktanks', to think up those new ideas; and with lobbyists and special advisors, to help provide the politicians with the ideas they don't have time to have (just so long as they don't appear to have been borrowed from anyone in particular).

And we love the heroic originals and the unique individuals who we think make these fresh new ideas: the Elvises and the Newtons, the Picassos and the Pullmans, the Brailsfords and his heroic bicycling protégés.

By contrast, copying feels wrong in a number of ways. For many in modern business, copying is theft, plain and simple. Jonathan Ives, the designer behind Apple's iPod, iPhone and iPad, puts it this way in complaining of his imitators: 'What's copied isn't just a design, it's thousands and thousands of hours of struggle. It takes years of investment, years of pain.'[14]

Big business's lawyers love finding ways to protect their clients' intellectual property, to stop other businesses copying their ideas and sunk costs. The London Olympics Organizing Committee even tried to copyright the words '2012', 'Olympic' and 'London'. It made economic sense to try – imagine how much the city of Paris could have earned on '1924' by now – even if these efforts made LOCOG look a little silly and money-grabbing.

Part of the problem here is the notion of copying as deception: deliberately presenting one thing as if it were another. Passing off somebody else's thing as if it was mine.

This whiff of the deception involved in copying runs deeper: copying has some more negative tones beyond the economic dimension. If you discover something's been copied from elsewhere, that thing seems to have less intrinsic value immediately.

> **❝ Discovering something is copied makes it seem less valuable. ❞**

So when you read Matt Bateman's critique of the plot of James Cameron's movie *Avatar*, it's hard not to think (even) less of the movie than you did previously. The huge number of similarities to the plot of the very successful Disney movie *Pocahontas* is hard to see as other than deliberate.

Perhaps this is a little unfair – after all, Bateman's plot synopsis of the two movies is written in such a way as to highlight the similarities between the two movies. He might just as easily have mentioned movies such as *Dances with Wolves* or even Kurasawa's *The Seven Samurai* as source material – both feature an outsider who comes to make friends with natives and ends up winning their confidence and taking the side against his own exploitative people. The New Zealand children's animated cartoon, *Fern Gully*, is visually even closer to *Avatar*: it features blue-skinned natives in a dense and inhospitable forest for the hero to make friends with.

Extract from *Pocahontas* (Disney) modified by Matt Bateman

Source: http://unrealitymag.com/index.php/2010/01/04/behold-the-tale-of-avatahontas/

> **There is no shame in copying good stories.**

To the anthropologist there is no shame in copying good stories: Joseph Campbell famously showed how the original *Star Wars* series of the 1970s and 1980s had its roots in classical mythology – plot motifs that have been favourites since *Little Red Riding Hood*, which is thousands of years old, as anthropologist Jamie Tehrani of Durham University has recently shown. Some details may vary but essentials are the same. For example, the Irish *Snow White* is called *Lasair Gheug*. In this version of the story, it is a little trout, rather than a mirror, who repeatedly tells the Evil Queen stepmother that she is not the most beautiful woman that ever was in Ireland. It is still essentially the same story.

But to my mind even knowing that there are these story archetypes doesn't make the feeling of less go away, really. It's disappointing when you learn that a particular thing isn't as unique and special as you thought it was.

We don't like copycats...at all.

When it comes to *people* who copy, that is when the confused feelings around copying start to become even clearer. We don't like copiers, at all.

I grew up preventing my school friends copying my work by judicious use of an extended arm and elbow (while simultaneously peering as well as I could at their answers).

Today's technology makes it much easier for students to copy the work of others. Indeed, many educationalists underline the importance of group- and peer-learning as methods to drive up learning in any group of students. At the same time, academics and schoolteachers have both had to find text-checking software to check for plagiarism (or 'cut-and-paste' writing, to be precise) in work submitted by students.

Similar tools and the 'wisdom of crowds', which digital media facilitates, make it hard for journalists and writers to get away with copying others' work as much as perhaps they used to, though some continue to persevere nobly – in journalism, the *New York Times*' Maureen Dowd and the *Toronto Globe* and *Mail*'s Margaret Wente have been at the centre of just two high profile cases of recent years. Indeed, while former *Wired* journalist and author Jonah Lehrer has admitted to fabricating interview quotes to make a better story (proper faking), I'm amused by the accusation thrown at him that he has self-plagiarized not just once but no less than 13 times[15] in various pieces.

'The more instances of duplicity we discover, the more it seems Lehrer devalues originality – the very thing we turn to him for. Had he stolen words from someone else – plagiarized-plagiarized rather than self-plagiarized – we'd all be calling it quits.'

THE REAL JOE BIDEN

Senator (now vice president) Joe Biden's first run for the democratic presidential nomination fell apart in 1987 when newspapers started to circulate rumours that Biden was a 'copier':[16] a high-profile and very well received speech he gave bore very strong resemblances to one given earlier that year by Neil Kinnock, then leader of the British Labour Party, about opportunity and social mobility. Here are the relevant portions of the two speeches:

'Why am I the first Kinnock in a thousand generations to be able to get to university? Was it because our predecessors were thick? Does anybody really think that they didn't get what we had because they didn't have the talent or the strength or the endurance or the commitment? Of course not. It was because there was no platform upon which they could stand.'

'Why is it that Joe Biden is the first in his family ever to go to a university? [Then pointing to his wife in the audience] Why is it that my wife who is sitting out there in the audience is the first in her family to ever go to college? Is it because our fathers and mothers were not bright? Is it because I'm the first Biden in a thousand generations to get a college and a graduate degree that I was smarter than the rest?'[17]

While Biden had frequently cited Kinnock as his source elsewhere, on two public occasions at least he failed to do so – the 21 August Democratic Debate at the Iowa State Fair and in an interview on 26 August for the National Education Association. This gave the impression to some that he was trying to pass off someone else's ideas as his own – a notion reinforced by the discovery that he'd previously quoted large chunks of Robert F. Kennedy and Hubert Humphrey without crediting them.

ME, MYSELF AND I

Part of our discomfort here is, I think, rooted in the sense of the other party deceiving us – consciously or otherwise – but I suspect that there's something else going on.

Our culture has a very strong individualist strand: we prize the individual over the group and distrust those who don't have a strong sense of authentic self, who don't 'know their own mind', 'self-actualize', 'sing their own song' or whatever metaphor is popular down the dark self-help aisle in the bookstore.

We are discomforted by the conformist and the copier who lack this authentic (for good or ill) core:

- Chameleon characters like Woody Allen's Zelig, who literally absorbed the physical and behavioural characteristics of those he spent time with, Nazi leaders included.
- Those who abide too closely by the rules of high school (teenage rebellion, yay!) or suburban country club (or union or whatever).
- Those who toe the party line too often – in politics or in the world more generally.
- Those who are easily led and those with weak wills or lack or self-confidence – all of these we look down on …

Our culture places a strong injunctive on individuals to be themselves. Those who don't are somehow failing. Oscar Wilde is the poster-boy for this when he suggests that:

'most people are other people: their thoughts someone else's opinions, their lives a mimicry, their passions a quotation'.

Individual identity and self-determination are central tenets of our contemporary culture. 'Just be yourself' the bumper sticker cries, 'Everyone else is taken'.

'WE' FICTION IS SCARY

Our fictions reveal the depth of this individualism and our dislike of those without a central core of self. This is where our love of heroes and villains is rooted – in some ways, we'd prefer it if people were genuinely good or bad – life would be much simpler. It's also why our stories of innovation are about the unusual and inventive individuals like Elvis and Newton, rather than the broader team involved in making new things.

We find the 'single white female' of the movie of the same name shocking – she copies the hair, dress and interests of her roommate, tries to steal her boyfriend by pretending to be the girl and then finally plots murder. Other fictions, such as *The Stepford Wives*, *Doctor Who*'s Daleks and Cybermen and the *Midwitch Cuckoos* and the plague of zombie stories that we're currently surrounded by, reveal quite how deep this fear about the lack of authentic individualism goes. When Gene Roddenberry's team were seeking a new mortal enemy for the all-American individualists on the *Starship Enterprise*, they specifically chose the Borg as the polar opposite: a Hive-Mind without a sense of personal self and originality. *What could be scarier to mainstream America?*

WEIRD

The individualist view of the world sees humanity as a species of 'individuals … tiny organisms with private lives … personal power, success and fame are the absolute measures of values, the things to live for'.[18] But when you look beyond the limits of Anglo-Saxon and American culture in particular, it's a point of view that is neither widely shared – though it may seem a self-evident truth to you and I – nor is it fact.

Rather, it is WEIRD, as in 'Western, educated, industrialized, rich and democratic' societies, the acronym coined by Joe Henrich and Ara Norenzyan. More and more social scientists are discovering that WEIRD societies (yes, that means us) are the anomalies in terms of our species across time and cultures. Indeed, it appears we may have been misled in many ways by what we have learned from scientific studies to describe as 'universal' human characteristics because the vast majority of psychological experiments and economic games have been conducted on WEIRD subjects like American university students.

> ## The vast majority of psychological experiments and economic games have been conducted on WEIRD subjects.

Many cross-cultural studies like psychologist Richard Nisbett's *The Geography of Thought* demonstrate that the aggressive individualism of Anglo-Saxon culture is not widely shared by other cultures. My own experience of working across non-Anglo Saxon cultures supports this strongly. Southern Africa has its notion of Ubuntu (connectedness and mutuality) which sees man as a fundamentally social being, rather than a 'host of individual entities that cannot help being in constant conflict'.[19] As Archbishop Desmond Tutu famously put it:

'my humanity is caught up and inextricably bound up in yours. A person with Ubuntu [has] a proper self-assurance that comes from knowing that they belong in a greater whole and are diminished when others are humiliated or diminished.'[20]

11

Swahili-speaking East Africa has the notion of Kiva which means much the same as Ubuntu. 'Us-together' not 'me and mine'.

Latin cultures, too, are more 'we' than 'me'. An evening spent in a small Italian or Spanish town will underline the centrality of peers and family to Latin life. It is almost unthinkable for young Italians to go out on their own or small groups; the 'passegiata' parade around the local square is something everyone indulges in, especially on holidays. Italian business often progresses by getting to know each other and their families over dinner (which often leaves Anglo Saxons feeling lost in gastronomic foreplay). When pitching a project its you, who you know and how you are connected to them matters intensely as a mark of suitability in these 'we' cultures.

French Professor Bernard Cova and his collaborators have gone so far as to identify what they call the 'Latin School of Societing' which contrasts strongly with the Anglo Saxon me-me-me culture through which most of us in marketing and the behavioural sciences swim (whether or not we were brought up in 'me' or 'we' culture, we learn 'me' as we learn those disciplines and their practices).

Cova also highlights the strong 'we' bias of other – more northerly – European cultures. For example, while the rest of us may tend to characterize Sweden's world view in terms of its social democratic politics (one version of more 'we' than 'me'), the culture itself has deeper 'we' roots, with longstanding social norms for moderation and not standing out from the average, which precede modern political structures and ethos. The word 'lagom' for example – often translated as 'just the right amount' or 'moderate' – is a turnkey word which opens up this central notion in Swedish culture. To Swedes, at least. To the Finns, 'sopiva' has a similar meaning.

Even to the Australians, whom comparative cultural studies often describe as located on the individualist scale halfway between the British Anglo-Saxons and their more extreme North American cousins, 'we-ness' often overruns 'me-ness'. Anyone in Oz who presents themselves as a 'tall poppy' – thinking themselves better in some way from their peers – deserves to be cut down. By contrast, mate-dom – being a good bloke in the company of others – is one of the highest things an Ozzie man can aspire to.

The point here is twofold: first, the individualist 'me' world view is far from universal – indeed most cultures do not share it. Second, these kinds of cultural assumption (axiom, maybe?) are hard to see around. Often they are so embedded in a place, a group or a discipline (e.g. psychology) that they just seem to be how things are. And this can hide the value and importance of phenomena like copying which is anathema to a particular worldview. If the world is made up individuals, their lone efforts and their special talents and characteristics, how can copying – using the brains of others – ever be good?

COPYING IS GOOD FOR YOU (AND ME)

Copying (or 'social learning' as the behavioural sciences have long called it) turns out to be one of our species' greatest gifts and one of the factors most responsible for our success.

It starts really early: as early as 42 minutes old, as Professor Andrew Meltzoff's milestone research demonstrated.[21] Meltzoff's experimental technique was simple:

- Hold a selected baby in your arms, look into its eyes.
- Make a clear facial gesture at the baby – by, say, sticking out your tongue or opening your mouth wide.
- Observe the baby's reactions and record them.

When repeated many times over – both for human infants across different cultures and for the offspring of our closest simian cousins[22] – this disconcertingly simple methodology created some powerful learning:

- We copy earlier.
- We copy better.
- We go on copying long after the initial buzz has gone and without reward.

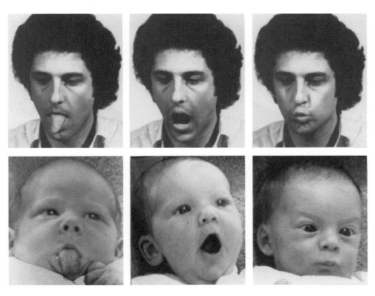

Source: 'Imitation of Facial and Manual Gestures by Human Neonates', Andrew N. Meltzoff and M. Keith Moore, *Science*, The American Association for the Advancement of Science, 7 October 1977. Reprinted with permission from AAAS.

If you have children yourself you know the truth of the great central importance of copying as THE learning style in human infants (they repeat the colourful language we use at home that we'd prefer no-one else – grandparent or teacher – to know about).

First they copy us, then their peers, then the media, then …

13

I'LL HAVE WHAT SHE'S HAVING

Sadly it doesn't stop at puberty (if only!). We grown-ups also use copying widely. Not least in the names we choose to give our children: my late mother always insisted that I was named 'Mark' after the thousands of times she had typed the words 'Deutschmark' and 'trademark' while pregnant with me (she was working as a translator at the time); however, it turns out that I am part of a cohort of British men whose parents all followed the short-lived fashion for 'Mark'.

> ## " We copy the choices and the behaviours of those around us. "

When faced with difficult situations or choices that are hard to tell apart, each of us *outsources the cognitive load* to those around us – we copy the choices and the behaviours of those around us. Whether it's in restaurants and bars (as demonstrated in *that* scene from *When Harry Met Sally*[23]), in voting booths, in the music we listen to, where we choose to live and the products we choose in the grocery store, we default to 'I'll have what she's having' more often than we'd imagine. Indeed, as the midterm review of the work of the UK Government's Behavioural Insights Team (the so-called 'nudge' unit) demonstrated, the biggest influence on an individual's behaviour (beyond what they've done previously) is what other people do and say.

For individual decision-makers, copying remains a pretty decent tactic for many situations, for many behaviours and for many choices.

NEUROLOGICALLY EFFICIENT

Moreover, 'I'll have what she's having' is pretty darn efficient, too. The kind of thinking that involves an individual in a considered weighing of options and calculating of probabilities is neurologically thirsty: it's slow and cumbersome because it soaks up a lot of processing power. And as a result, we often default to heuristics – like 'what I did last time' (copying your past self) or 'what everyone else is doing' (copying what's being done by others right now).

Nobel Laureate Daniel Kahneman[24] describes this considered style as 'System 2 thinking' – propositional, logic- and fact-based. By contrast, 'System 1 thinking' is much faster because it uses short-hands like 'what I did before', 'what everyone else is doing' and so on (indeed the ratio of processing speeds of the two kinds of approach has been calculated at 1:220). Human beings are to System 2 thinking, he says, like cats are to swimming – we can do it if we really have to but, like our feline friends, we will tend to avoid having to do it if we can.

"Copying is incredibly useful – it's quick, it's easy and it gets results."

No wonder then that 'copying' is so prevalent in human behaviour and seems to have been for as long as we have been human. Cognitive scientist Alex Mesoudi and anthropologist-archaeologist Michael O'Brien created an ingenious experiment, in which participants played a computer game of making spear-points designed to hunt bison. The participants were allowed to change aspects of the shape of the stone points – length, width, edge angles and so forth – and then see how well their point would perform (based on archaeological knowledge) on hunting actual bison. After each round, these 'hunters' could see their own scores in comparison with the scores and different designs that others were hunting with. Each hunter could invent new shapes, or copy others whose hunting-success scores they could see. In all runs of the game, social learners scored better than those who refused to copy others' success.

Work by other social scientists points in much the same direction: for example, in the software-based tournament created by Kevin Laland[25] and his team at St Andrews University, in which they were able to simulate the effect of large numbers of individuals (represented by a simple piece of code) interacting with each other of many iterations.

Laland and colleagues expected the winner would have a sophisticated 'social learning strategy' about whom and when to copy. Mere random copying was not seen as likely to win, 'because information may be wrong, and can become outdated'. The winners, in as much a surprise to themselves as to the expert panel overseeing the tournament, were two Canadian post-grads Dan Cownden (a neuroscientist) and Tim Lillicrap (a mathematician), neither of whom were social learning experts. They labelled their entry 'discount machine' – its basic instruction being to copy often, and to bias that copying towards recent successful strategies – 'discounting' the older information. It was not quite random copying, but close – copy any success, just as long as it is recent.

Copying then is incredibly useful to individuals in their immediate decision-context – it's quick, it's easy and it gets results. But it has much more important advantages for individuals, larger populations and the species as a whole.

WE-THINK

Any population of a social species like ours, who have the ability of individuals to learn (copy) from those around them, has a number of advantages over one in which copying is not so developed. It allows individuals to outsource all kinds of cognitive activity to those around them. From where the food is, to what's good to eat, who's

important and who's not, whether danger is emerging and how you get those yummy ants out of a log (or whatever).

Think of it this way: together – at a family party or reunion – we remember better than most of us can on our own. Copying is central to this ability to access the minds of others. Or in a football crowd, even with your eyes shut, you can tell when a goal has been scored, from the screaming and movement of all those around you.

❝ Copying is central to our ability to access the minds of others. ❞

PHONE A FRIEND

Copying, however, does something even more fantastic – it provides us with a knowledge and know-how bank that makes independent thought even less necessary in our everyday lives. Something we call 'culture'.

Take, for example, the way you (and most people who've grown up in European culture) tend to lay food out on individual plates: three kinds of thing, taking up roughly equal space – protein, carbohydrate and something called 'vegetables'. This is far from an obvious arrangement – indeed, many other cultures have a very different way of sorting food out. Italian meals can often

pull out the carbs to a separate course and Indian 'thalis' are shared dishes which sit between those eating together rather than in front of an individual. Nor is the current status quo fixed: we Northern Europeans have had very different arrangements in the past. For example, until the 18th Century the idea of cutlery was distinctly underdeveloped – the knife playing the same singular role it had already played for millennia. The fork by contrast arrived in France from Italy with Catherine de Medici in the 1540s and only became commonplace across the continent and in Britain in the 18th Century.

Flavour preferences and styles of cooking have also changed over time. Two generations ago it would have been inconceivable that Britain's most popular dish was an Indian curry (chicken tikka masala) or that one of the fastest growing food styles of the last decade would be raw fish (sushi). These are clearly behaviours that we have learned from those who learned from others who are now long gone: copying connects not just one individual to another but on and on over space and – importantly – over time.

Copying allows us to build this kind of coherent web of connections and store knowledge, information and know-how in them – which is what 'culture' really is. To phone a friend, if you like (even if they are a long time dead). The software community gets this – the fact that individual coders' work available to others enables more robust and interoperable code to be deployed more quickly. Why DIY?

iSPREAD

Copying is thus a central to how information, ideas and behaviour spread through populations. The modern world is full of examples: technology enables copying to happen at the press of a button and at the same time can often provide us with the means to track and understand it.

Take for example a simple news story: on the I-75, outside Monroe, Ohio, is the Solid Rock Church, long known to locals as 'the church of Touchdown Jesus' due to the unmissable (to anyone on the I-75) 62 ft tall, 16000 pound Styrofoam and fibreglass stature of Our Good Lord in a pose which makes it appear as if he's scored in the final seconds of the Superbowl.

On Monday June 14th 2010, however, the statue was struck by lightning. People – gossipy godless people like myself – love this kind of story. The nascent social platform, twitter, captured instantly how the news spread (as the graph shows). First, we see a spike of mentions that grows very rapidly and then declines, then subsequently a smoother and rounder growth.

'King of Kings' image by Joe Shlabotnik, reproduced under Creative Commons licence https://creativecommons.org/licenses/by/2.0/

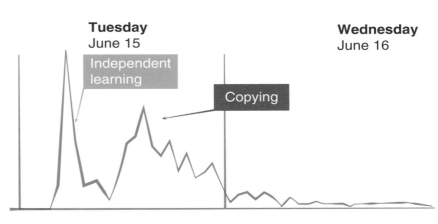

How to interpret this? Classic diffusion science is a big help in making sense of the twitter data (see Classic Diffusion Curves graph below). The spiky asymmetric curve on the left indicates that people here are acting independently (and in the case of Touchdown Jesus in response to the same external stimulus, the local news media). The rounder curve on the right (which you may recognize from Marketing 101 as a classic adoption curve) suggests that individuals are responding to other individuals – copying – rather than to the news story itself. And while the left hand 'independent' curve seems to reach much higher (many more people), it's the area under the curves we should compare – the right hand curve has more than 10x the people involved.

Similar patterns are clear from a study of all kinds of media content – how from articles in *The Economist* get popular, the success of movie and video game releases to the simple blog post or an embarrassing faux pas on twitter or Facebook which our politicians seem to love sharing with us. Put simply, if something doesn't have the copying – the social diffusion curve – it doesn't spread.

We see the same thing in the fads and 'memes' that dominate much of the online social world: in spread of the fun stuff (videos of babies or cats) and of the serious ('#jesuischarlie' and '#yeswecan'). And of course, the same thing is true (and has always been true) offline too. How do names become more or less popular, if not by copying? How did tennis pros develop the habit of the fist pump before and after every point? And everyone else who plays the game down on their local park courts?

However, copying doesn't just spread new things; it can also keep things the same and do so for surprisingly long periods. For example, the Neolithic longhouse was the product of hundreds of years of tight copying, with only the very occasional accident (or 'innovation' as Neolithic architects might call it) to create variation. Sometimes this

CLASSIC DIFFUSION CURVES

Independent Choice

Social influence

Diffusion through a population by individuals discovering the superior qualities of the product independently of their peers

Diffusion through a population by individuals mostly learning from each other either about the quality of the product or its social value is due to functional characteristics (the basic design worked pretty damn well) but more often it is because it becomes 'what we do round here' – a cultural practice that goes unquestioned.

What's more, a novel idea often takes a long time to get widely adopted – as it often has to replace something else. You'd be very lucky to find evidence of the transition from roundhouse to longhouse. This happened very slowly over tens of generations and at different speeds in different parts of Europe. This point will turn out to be important when you try and spread new behaviours or choices later on in the book: copying can also bolster the status quo and keep things as they are. That said, the modern world gives us so much access to so many other people (both in our immediate networks and beyond) that it can't help but fuel the creation of novelty.

So even when something new does arise, its spread is often largely due to copying of one sort or another. Or indeed its failure to spread is due to the population copying some other behaviour.

Ask yourself this: how did you ever buy this book? Or join twitter or Facebook? Or learn the jargon of your workplace? Or the slang of your peers? Or get your name? Or Elvis get his and I get mine?

CONCLUSION

- Copying is a really central part of what it is to be human.
- Copying helps us to make decisions quickly, easily and neurologically efficiently. And good ones at that, most of the time.
- Copying helps us navigate the broader world by using the brains and bodies of others – both those in front of us and those just beyond them; on out over space and time.
- Copying helps us learn new ideas and pass them on to our neighbours and their neighbours and so on.
- Copying is such an amazing and fundamentally human skill.

Yet, our Anglo-Saxon culture is blinded to the value of copying:

- We stigmatize it.
- We dislike it.
- We hide it and deny it.

But we don't have to – most humans on the planet and most humans who've ever lived, are perfectly at ease with copying, if done well (or badly, as we'll see). Elvis was. His tailor was. The team at the Elvies are. I am.

Want to learn how to use copying to make new stuff? Discover some more practical tools and approaches? Uncover some more 'how' and little less 'why'? That's the next chapter.

"Nothing is original. Steal from anywhere that resonates with inspiration or fuels your imagination. Devour old films, new films, music, books, paintings, photographs, poems, dreams, random conversations, architecture, bridges, street signs, trees, clouds, bodies of water, light and shadows... Authenticity is invaluable; originality is non-existent."

—Jim Jarmusch[26]

What this chapter will cover:

This chapter is more practical than the last: it will help you understand HOW to use copying to make new, original and more effective strategies and ideas.

We'll show how error and variation are good and useful.

We'll explore how who you copy from and where can create error and value.

_____

*Yes, I know. Showing my age.

We'll suggest games, techniques and examples to put all of this to work.

And why *what kinda thing*? questions are often more useful than more specific ones.

But first, '*more songs about buildings and food*'[27]*

2 HOW TO COPY WELL

Good, bad, tight, loose, close or far away

A RACE TO THE TOP

The British-Iranian architect Zaha Hadid is undoubtedly one of the cultural rock stars of the modern world. Her elegant and striking buildings, with their characteristically simple flowing organic forms, regularly win awards and media plaudits in equal measure.

Having a 'Hadid' is great box office, whether or not your development is commercial, civic or some version of the two. So when London's Serpentine Gallery sought to extend the 19th-Century neoclassical Magazine Building overlooking the Serpentine Lake in the heart of Hyde Park, Hadid's very 21st-Century curtain of smooth tensile materials which seem to embrace and engulf the boxy Regency solidity, proved – at least after the fact – a natural choice for this very 'look-at-me' development.

Of all the buildings that were put up to populate the 2012 Olympic village in East London, none was as memorable or as striking as Hadid's Aquatic Centre with its wave-like form echoing the activity inside.

More recently however, Hadid has found herself entangled in a surreal race to finish the construction of one of her buildings before a copy of that building is completed, in the same country.

COPYING ORIGINALS

Like many star architects of her generation, Hadid has been lured to China by the scale and the bravery of the developments being put together during the largest property boom of living memory. Nowhere is her status more apparent than in China: she has a dozen or so projects in various stages of construction across the People's Republic, including the incredibly beautiful Guangzhou Opera House (completed in 2010).

But the striking design she has created for the billionaire property developer Zhang Xin in the Galaxy SOHO development in the heart of Beijing – five continuously flowing volumes which enclose a traditional Chinese courtyard – is being simultaneously copied in Chongqing (a new city out on the edge of the Tibetan plain) 'even as we build one of Zaha's projects'.

While there are differences – in scale and shape – between the two buildings, they are clearly two versions of the same blueprint – two peas from the same pod. One is clearly a copy – not an 'homage', a 'response' or a 'tribute to' the other. Why would somebody do this so blatantly, particularly of the work of such a high profile architect?

" Why would you copy a building? "

Copying the style of buildings you admire is nothing new. Throughout history, architects have done so (more on how in Chapter 4). From the classicists who sought inspiration (aka source materials) in Ancient Greek and Roman temples – why should The Bank of England look like a Roman Palace? To those seeking a feeling for the exotic – the residence built for the erstwhile Prince Regent in 18th Century Brighton looks like a theatre set for a show about the White Rajahs (which is what it is essentially). Ditto the fantastical palace of dreams built at NeuSchwanstein in Bavaria for the unfortunate King Ludwig II, including the installation of twinkling lights above the royal bed, to suggest a (dramatic) hero's sleep beneath the stars.

In the 19th Century Baron Haussmann reshaped the centre of historic Paris, laying out the broad boulevards, squares and tall, elegant buildings in the French classical style (borrowed again from the Ancients) that we now think of as essentially Parisian. This in turn influenced in various ways those who sought to reshape and modernize other world cities – Rome, Vienna, Stockholm, Madrid and Barcelona.

But replicating whole buildings or whole towns in detail with even any pretence at adaptation? Well, in China at least this is far from unheard of. In the northern city of Tianjin, a 15th-Century fishing village has been obliterated by a replica of the Manhattan skyline, with its own reproduction Rockefeller Centre and fake Hudson River. In Zhengzhou, a copy of Corbusier's Ronchamp chapel was erected in the1990s (until protests from France and Corbusier's Foundation got it pulled down). Copies of European landmarks such London's Tower Bridge and Paris' Tour Eiffel are to be found in Suzhou and Tianducheng respectively. More recently, a copy of the entire alpine town of Halstatt – itself a UNESCO world heritage site and major tourist destination – sprouted up in Guangdong province, much to the consternation of the Austrian original and its Federal Government. No such worries or howls of pain from Londoners however: Thames Town replete with mock Tudor stylings and gothic spires first appeared in Sionjiang district some 30 miles from Shanghai back in 2006.

BAD COPYING?

For many years, Asian countries have been particularly keen to copy Western products and manufacturing techniques

and technology, in order to learn how to do them better. Think of how the Japanese and the Koreans have gone from being the producers of cheap copies of European and American electronics to dominating many of those industries. Today, however, the Chinese have a particular expertise in this practice and have coined a special word to describe it 'Shanzai' (from 'bandit fortress' – somewhere beyond the reach of the law – and Shenzen where many of the sweatshops cranking this stuff out were originally based).

Shanzai products continue to pour out of Chinese factories to serve the tastes and budgets of the 1.3 billion new consumers (especially the 60% of the population who live in the newer and more remote cities and rural locations).

It would be wrong to consider these Shanzai products as inferior per se, as you might be tempted to do: many are just as good, if not better than the originals on which they are based. For example, some 10-20% of the world's smartphones are believed to be Shanzai – no name devices with the same touch-screen, mp3, game and video playing capabilities. They can often have some additional features, too, like a double- or triple-Sim-card slot (the reliability of mobile networks in many Chinese cities is legendary, so who wouldn't want an extra option or two?). All at a fraction of the cost of the original.

So how do you tell them apart? Well probably the best clue for a native English speaker lies in the brand names – 'Naik' (Nike) sneakers or 'Dolce and Banana' (D&G) shirts and luggage. That said, I'm not sure I'd feel that confident eating at Mek Dek or Buckstars.

> ## " Some 10-20% of the world's smartphones are Shanzai. "

SHANZAI APPLE?

And no brand is immune. When blogger BirdAbroad[28] spotted a fake Apple store in the city of Kunming in the south-western corner of the People's Republic, the Apple corporation was far from pleased, but absolutely not surprised.

Again, the quality differences weren't the clue to the fakery – the interiors, the décor, the products and the merchandising all conformed to the brand's standard practices in other cities and the staff seemed convinced that they worked for the kosher organization. The difference was to be seen in tiny details or one tiny detail in particular: BirdAbroad noted that the signage referred to the store as 'Apple Store' which is a term that the corporation never uses in retail signs.

The giveaway details included using PCs to calculate payments.

As it happens, subsequent investigations revealed there were actually five (!) fake Apple stores in the one city, with varying degrees of fidelity to the Jobs/Ives' design template. Two were quickly closed by the authorities because they didn't seem to have business licences, but the others remained open despite strong opposition from the corporation (although they have been told by local authorities to stop using the Apple logo).

Fake Apple stores continue to flourish in a number of Chinese cities – for example, in Lincang some seven hours to the north of Kunming there are several fake stores which only give themselves away by small details – staff t-shirts with iron-on logos and tills which (ahem…) use PCs to calculate payments. The products themselves seem to be genuine – insiders suggest that they may be by-products of the Apple contract manufacturing businesses in China (surplus stock or deliberate production overruns).

SINGLE WHITE COPYING

Seen from an innovator's point of view, Shanzai primarily represents the bad and not the good side of copying: it seeks to exploit the intellectual and financial effort involved in making something new and better (cue the IP lawyers). This is where many of our ideas about the deceitfulness and unfairness of the copycat are rooted.

Single White Copying (see the Introduction) is no good to the innovator because it doesn't create novelty – it just repeats the same thing endlessly. And as in the movie of the same name, it can just feel a little bit spooky.

Single White Copying is no good for innovation.

One well-known (and really unhelpful) example of this kind of copying is the widespread management consultancy practice of benchmarking. This tool was first introduced in the 1980s to the Xerox Corporation and is widely credited for successfully reinventing that organization after a rapid

and massive drop in US market share (from 100% to 14%) in the aftermath of the tricky purchase of Western Union and a hostile anti-trust ruling.

Benchmarking was originally intended as a way to enable a company to compare how it allocates its resources with how its competitors do so (in order to ensure that it wasn't wasting money paying over the odds for some ingredient or component). However, in practice, benchmarking quickly became an excuse to bring all supply chain costs on par with competitors.

For example, McKinsey[29] have described how when the different companies in the German Telco industry all adopted this kind of practice (matching each others' manufacturing costs and practices through something called 'value-chain analysis') they effectively destroyed value in that market in a matter of months.

For both consumers (as a result of increadingly homogenised offers) and business (in terms of the resulting reduced profitability from greater price-point competition and lack of differentiation).

Used in this way, tight copying can be a disaster.

IN-BETWEENIES

How can this be? One of the best ways to explore similar – sometimes abstract – phenomena is through games using human participants. A few years ago, two academic experts on crowd behaviour, Professor Jens Krause (a zoologist who first came to my attention with his experiments on shoaling behaviour in sticklebacks using a 'robofish' mechanical interloper) and Professor Dirk Helbing (whose work on human crowd behaviour and self-organizing systems leads the field) collaborated for a programme rooted in game play for German TV which demonstrated how various crowd phenomena emerge.

Our game is much simpler and demonstrates what happens at scale in a population when a crowd copy each other too closely. I call it 'In-betweenies'.

First, I gather a crowd of 15-20 (more is fine, but less can make the game run very fast – too fast to observe what's going on).

Second, I ask them to walk around randomly but to avoid bumping into each other. This serves to spread them evenly through the room.

Third, I ask them to stop and – without saying or doing anything to indicate their choice – to choose a friend (F) and an enemy (E).

Fourth, I ask all the individuals to move again but – just as you might expect in real life – their job now becomes keeping between their friend (F) and their enemy (E). At all costs.

Very quickly, this is what happens:

Everyone ends up in the same space in one big ball.

It's not hard to see why: the tightness of the relationship we have enforced between individual agents means that they all end up clumped. In marketing terms, read 'undifferentiated'.

WE TRY EVEN HARDER

But don't be mistaken: increasingly it's clear that Shanzai can offer the platform for innovation.

Take, for example, a Shanzai business like eHi. While Hertz and Avis have struggled to embed their US-based car-hire business model into mainland China (in pursuit of the sniff of billions of dollars pouring into the Chinese automotive market), eHi copied and then innovated.

To an aspiring Chinese executive sitting in the gridlocked traffic in China's great cities (and on the vehicle clogged highways out to the blossoming suburbs which now surround them I suspect), self-drive car hire can seem less than appealing: real status is now signalled by having someone take the strain of driving you around.

eHi offer both chauffeur-driven and self-drive options (and the chauffeur-driven option is increasingly popular, now accounting for more than 50% of eHi's revenue). Only eHi were alert to the need to adapt the US model for Chinese consumers; Avis and Hertz have been too concerned with optimizing their existing model to listen to and observe their new customers.

So copying can make things better. It's in this spirit that Zaha Hadid seems to welcome the copying of her work even before it is finished – despite the obvious frustrations around the race to complete her SOHO Galaxy building before its Shanzai version topped out – on the basis that the copy might come up with better or different technological solutions to the construction, then 'that would be interesting'.

> ## " What better way to beat the copycats than copying back? "

Smart Western companies are also wising up to this potential for Shanzai to point up innovations: Nokia, Apple and Microsoft all engage anthropologists to report back on Shanzai innovations in their developing markets. After all – what better way to beat the copycats but to use them to suggest innovations that you can then copy?

INVENTION AND INNOVATION

This style of copying is itself far more common than you'd imagine. Indeed, in the academic disciplines of anthropology and archaeology (which have the advantage of a longer-term perspective on how technologies and designs spread and evolve over time), *invention* (the creation of a radically new thing) is seen as something entirely different from *innovation* (the slow process of evolution of a class of thing through repeated copying and variation): the latter being far more common and pervasive than the former.

Most of us lean too heavily on the former (indeed, we tend to use the word 'innovation' when we mean 'invention', don't we?). Who wouldn't want to be responsible for making a new thing rather just a version of somebody else's new thing?

The great economist Shumpeter famously distinguished between having an idea and getting it adopted: 'Innovation is the market introduction of a technical or organisational novelty, not just its invention'.[30] He was very clear on the superior value of 'innovation' in this sense: what matters is not having a new idea (those are ten a penny) but taking an idea to market; making it happen is where the juice is. Theodore Levitt concurred: 'Ideas are useless unless used'. George RR Martin (yes, the *Game of Thrones* man again) agrees: 'Ideas are cheap. I have more ideas now than I could ever write up. To my mind, it's the execution that is all-important.'[31]

" Innovation is more important than invention. "

ORIGINALITY DOESN'T PAY

Indeed, most studies suggest that genuine originality rarely pays as much as copying. No-one remembers the original fast-food chain (White Castle) but everybody knows

McDonald's who copied their ideas, systems and philosophy. Back in the 1960s, marketing guru Theodore Levitt acknowledged this, pointing out that the best-selling 'glamour mag' of the era, *Playboy*, was a rip-off of earlier titles.

And – whatever the IP lawyers say – few of Apple Corporation's so-called 'innovations' (mp3 players, icon-based interfaces, touch-screens, tablets, etc.) were real 'inventions'. Indeed, since the initial failure of the Newton, one of the most important rules of operation that Apple learned was not to be first to any market.

The facts bear this out: creators don't benefit that much from their work – typically getting less that 7% of the market value over its lifetime. As *The Economist* put it recently, it's learning from other businesses, rather than hard-core innovation, that really separates the sheep from the goats.

Anthropologists and archaeologists generally look over the longer term and across different populations. Indeed these disciplines tend to see the invention of a genuinely new thing – whether deliberate or by accident (as in Elvis' rockabilly sound) – as a really very rare phenomenon in human populations. So rare that it's far better to think of 'innovation' as not-inventing something but as some form of copying. Which is what we do most of the time anyway.

KEEP CALM

A highly visible example of this kind of iterative 'innovation' is the 'Keep Calm' meme that has spread and seeped in recent years into every corner of British culture (yes, mugs, aprons and politics).

In 1939, as the British Government waited for the inevitable mass bombing campaigns on British cities following the anticipated outbreak of war, the Ministry of Information prepared a series of inspirational propaganda posters and pamphlets to manage the morale of the population at large.

The first two posters in the series 'Freedom Is In Peril. Defend It With All Your Might' and 'Your Courage, Your Cheerfulness, Your Resolution Will Bring Us Victory' were printed and deployed but the 250,000 copies of 'Keep Calm and Carry On' were only given scant public exposure and disappeared from view rapidly after that.

Until 2000 that is, when Stuart and Mary Manley of Barter Books in Alnwick, Northumberland found an original in a consignment of used books they had bought at auction. They framed the print and put it behind the till in their shop and soon – following repeated customer requests – they started printing copies, featuring the Tudor crown and the classic sans typeface. The phrase started to appear on posters, on cards, on mugs and on t-shirts and as it started to spread so subtle

changes emerged as the idea seeped into different areas of popular culture.

Variations include pop band McFly's 'Keep Calm and Play Louder' tour, Matt Jones'[32] 'Get Excited and Make Things' (with cross spanners in place of the crown) and 'Keep Calm and Hate Microsoft' (or 'Apple' depending on which tech community you belong to).

Even local politics adopted the phrase: in 2012/13, the Save Lewisham Hospital Campaign made widespread use of a poster featuring the line 'Don't Keep Calm Get Angry and Save Lewisham A&E'.

Dr Hiroshi Hitake's mug in Season 1 of TV show *Helix* brandishes the original line, while my own favourite adaptation is topical for English cricket fans everywhere: 'Keep Calm and Bat On', something we need more and more of, it must be said.

The full story is told in a lovely documentary by StudioCanoe, called *Keep Calm And Carry On*[33] but if you just want to make your own, the 'Keep Calm-o-Matic' website will help you do so.

Now many of these variations are pretty poor – as is often the case with this kind of error-strewn copying – but some (including those suggested above) are novel and interesting things in their own right. And it turns out it's the error that matters.

 CHANGE WORDS AND BE HILAROUS

 I CAN'T KEEP CALM SO EXCITED!

 KEEP CALM AND FOLLOW JESUS!

 KEEP CALM AND LISTEN TO MUSIC

KEEP CALM AND BAT ON

KEEP CALM AND MAKE STUFF!

 KEEP CALM AND LOVE MARMITE

 KEEP CALM AND DRINK TEA

 KEEP CALM AND GO FISHING

 KEEP CALM AND LOVE A BEAR

 KEEP CALM AND DRINK BEER

 FREAK OUT AND RUN AWAY!

 KEEP CALM AND MIND YOUR OWN BUSINESS

 KEEP CALM AND CARRY ON

 KEEP CALM AND ROCK ON

 KEEP CALM and DRINK WINE

 KEEP CALM AND MAKE LOVE

 KEEP CALM AND GO SHOPPING

Source: Images sourced from http://www.keepcalm-o-matic.co.uk

MAKING DELIBERATE COPYING ERRORS

Pop-artist Andy Warhol is probably best known for his prints of iconic individuals (from Marilyn Monroe to Mao Tze Tung), often heavily re-coloured and printed many times (a wall of ten Maos being one of my favourites). So iconic have these prints become that you can now have your family photographs reprinted in this style by your local print shop.

Many discussions of the meaning and significance of Warhol's art concentrate on what his repeated reproduction of found images (most of his prints are based on existing photographs) suggests about originality in the age of mass reproduction. However, what has always attracted me is how he makes new from old, how each and every print is different even if the same colours are used in the same format.

An ever-so-slightly off-kilter impression of ink on paper could be seen as an error, but in most cases it adds to the uniqueness of the print itself. Each episode of printing creates novelty: the error in reproduction is where the juice lies. Accidental innovation you might call it.

Fortunately, most human copying is looser than the semi-mechanical reproduction that lies behind even Warhol's print-making.

CHINESE WHISPERS

Human copying is often more like a game of physical Chinese whispers (or 'broken telephone' game, for US readers). My colleagues and I often play this game with clients and audiences at our seminars and workshops.

On the page opposite you can see how this plays out. We line participants up, all facing in the same direction and staring at the back of the head of the person in front of them. This game, we explain, is all about copying what you see. But wait until you are tapped on the shoulder, then and only then turn round. A show and tell in a line, if you like…

MAKING ERROR

If you continue the game along a line of, say, a dozen players, the initial gesture(s) are always transformed to a significant degree, albeit little-by-little, sometimes slow, sometimes more rapidly. Insignificant copying error by insignificant copying error. I often ask participants and observer to describe what they're seeing: all too readily, the idea of 'error' emerges in a negative sense – as if the goal was to replicate the behaviour along the line. As in, 'so-and-so got it 'wrong' or 'they didn't copy right'. I find the default value-judgement here striking: error is bad. Well of course it is if you think copying is of the Single White ('tight') Female kind rather than the innovator's friend, looser copying. The former seeks to replicate, the latter to create error and variation. The former keeps things the same, the latter creates novelty to something pre-existing via making error. Just like Elvis and the boys created their sound by mucking about in Chapter 2. Make more error – it's good for you and your innovation.

> ❝ **Make more error – it's good for you and your innovation.** ❞

Step 1 First, we ask the individual at the back of the line to tap the person directly in front of them on the shoulder. The latter turns round and watches the simple gesture made by the initiatior (I normally suggest 3 simple hand or body movements but for this example, we've simplified).

Step 2 Now it's the turn of the second player to tap the person in front of them on the shoulder and repeat the show (or what they thought is the show).

Step 3 Now the third player gets to tap the person in front of them and show them what they've just seen from second player (the one behind). Players one and two watch.

Step 4 By this time, it's quite clear to the audience and those players who have already had their turn that the gesture(s) going along the line is changing and evolving. An exaggerated movement or a left-right switch or change in order.

ERROR AND EXCELLENCE

Illustrations reproduced with permission of Jonathan Tremlett

One bright spring morning, more than 30 years ago, I found myself clambering up the steps to the Matisse museum at Cimiez, high above the Provençal City of Nice. With the smell of pines, wild rosemary and mimosa in the air all around, I stepped inside the rather grand villa which sits perched above the Mediterranean, admiring the searing colours of the paintings and the great cut-out pictures of the artist's latter years – the sharpness and brutal cleanliness of the contrasts. Above all, the bright, bright blues.

But when I think back now, what I remember most of all is the line of bronze busts of his beloved wife Jeannette.

This line of sculptures of the same woman in the same pose (but cast over six or seven years from 1910 onwards) shows the progression of an artist's ability to represent the human

form, from the highly naturalistic to twisted, cubist. Each item a deliberate variation of the last.

High-end milliner Justin Smith – the man behind Angelina Jolie's striking twin horned headwear in the Disney movie *Malificient* – stitches hats by hand: he uses old fashioned cast-iron pressing machinery and wooden lasts (moulds). While each hat of a certain batch is based on the same last, each is inevitably different from both stitching AND pressing. His new 'black' collection features 50 different styles but each will vary over time in the material he uses, rather than the style.

Interestingly, he can also claim to be the author of that specific hat style which is now commonplace in hipster land – hats with cat ears sewn into them have been copied and recopied by all and sundry and evolved into bear, dog and even fox ears.

34

COPY: 'KOPERIEN', 'NACHMACHEN' OR 'ABKUFERN'

The art of translation is dogged by these kinds of errors and associated questions: a great translation is far more than information converted from one language to another, as a machine might imagine it.

> ## " A great translation is far more than information converted from one language to another. "

Hemingway is great in both English and German but different in each. Wieland's 1765 translation of *Hamlet* from English to German is a different thing to the original English language text, but valued as highly by many generations of German readers.

Irish poet Seamus Heaney's award-winning translation of the Anglo-Saxon *Beowolf* into modern English is more than a transcription from the ancient to the modern – it is an inspired work in its own right, with variation creating something both different and at the same time closer to the original.

Similarly, in the extraordinary chain-translation experiment that is *Multiples*: 12 Stories in 18 Languages by 61 authors, each contributor subtly changing the story told by their predecessor – each rendering a fresh translation, a fresh retelling of the same story. Weaving in and out of English, authors such as Zadie Smith and Jeffrey Eugenides, Laurent Binet and Javier Marías, David Mitchell and Colm Tóibín show how novelty is created through the telling and retelling of the same story. This is what happens in the real world with stories, rumours and even 'objective fact' – novelty arises through copying.

Another angle of how copying can create new work through variation is illustrated by former Poet Laureate Andrew Motion's recent award-winning work, *Chapter House*. Here, Motion creates a kind of poetic collage of WWI experiences, using not only the work of the recognized 'war poets' (Sassoon, Brooke etc.) but also the letters and correspondence of ordinary infantrymen. The result is an entirely new poetic evocation of the experience of war, and at the same time, one rooted in copying.

CUT-UPS

Sometimes, you have to use specific techniques to create variation from pre-existing materials. David Bowie's best song-writing is based on just this. From *Diamond Dogs* onwards – the first album in which he used the 'cut-up' (and re-assemblage) technique pioneered by the cult

author William Burroughs and his collaborator Brion Gysin. In essence this involves taking a linear text and cutting it up into words and phrases then reassembling to make new sense. If Bowie had based both the Ziggy Stardust character and his world partly at least on Burroughs' 1971 *Wild Boys* novel, then cut-ups provided a variation engine that made the most of the 15 years after he killed Ziggy off – Bowie's creative peak. Cut-ups are a very good loose-copying tool for lyricists.

Early in his masterpiece on the world of craft and work,[34] sociologist and philosopher Richard Sennett explores the history of medieval guilds. He demonstrates that while the way they organized themselves tended to create abiding notions of quality and craftsmanship (through tight copying of a small number of practitioners in a particular location under strict supervision of the guild's leaders), the fact that craftsmen were also encouraged to travel created the opportunity for looser copying – for novelty to emerge and spread.

Sennett cites the great Arab proto-sociologist Ibn Khaldun, who travelled in Spanish Andalusia studying 'the wares of local Christian guilds, as well as the work of itinerant goldsmiths. The goldsmiths seem to him like Berbers, made strong by travel and mobility. Sedentary guilds, by contrast, appeared … inert and "corrupt". The good master, in his words, "presides over a travelling house".' Which roughly translates as the good master ensures that the copying in his house is 'loose' as well as 'tight'.

COPYING LOOSELY CAN BE DANGEROUS

That said, the ability of copying to create error is not always a good thing. You may remember one particularly high-profile example which caused the Challenger Space Shuttle disaster: the Shuttle itself had been manufactured and transported to the launch site in two parts. This unusual construction method meant that NASA's engineers had to understand and calibrate the risk of launch failure under different weather conditions, especially the kind of cold snap that the launch date enjoyed. In particular, the 'o-rings' that connected the two parts of the reassembled launch rocket together were prone to freezing and thereby failure.

> **The ability of copying to create error is not always a good thing.**

So while the engineers and scientists knew that launching under these conditions was likely to be risky, their very objective knowledge was modulated as it went up and down (and up and down and up and down and up again) through the organization until – some days after the original launch date had passed – when the information had been degraded again and again through copying and recopying, the OK was given to proceed. The consequence was that the Shuttle exploded on take-off, killing all crew members instantly.

" Unless you train your human links, they will inevitably create variation. "

We tend nowadays to think that the only good kind of network is an open one: one in which all the nodes are able to make their own decisions and take or add as they please. But the example above shows the dangers of not accounting for this 'natural' feature of many social networks.

In the field of Emergency Response Planning, this is also the case. Imagine that the country is faced with some overwhelming phenomenon (an incident at a nuclear installation, a terrorist attack or an epidemic of e.g. SARS),

the successful transmission of information through the back up network and the adoption of specific responses is what's wanted; the last thing the emergency planners need is nodes in their information 'going rogue' and making up their own mind about what to do, what to record, what to pass on to the network.

A great deal of time and energy goes in to training those involved in keeping us safe from these kinds of foreseeable threats to *not* think – to do merely what they have been trained to do. In other words, to act more like a simple switch in a circuit than the kind of hero Hollywood might want: if this happens, do A; if this other thing happens, do B. Don't think, don't try to be clever, just respond precisely in the way we need you to.

According to the professionals in the field I've spoken to, it's remarkably hard to get people to be the dumb nodes in a network that will minimize the error in information transmitted around it; to keep copying-induced noise out of the system and the signal bright and clear. Unless you train your human links to do so (and get them practicing regularly) they will inevitably introduce variation and error again.

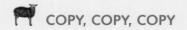

COPYING AND EVOLUTION

By contrast, Charles Darwin has the sense of the central and very positive role of copying and the variations it creates at the heart of his *Theory of Evolution*.[35]

When Darwin's name appears, most of us jump straight to the notion of the survival of the fittest (the idea that fitness of the individual or individual trait for a given environment is what makes it successful – the 'fittest' individuals are 'selected', we say, by that environment and this is what explains their long-term survival and thriving).

Just like the great man's contemporaries, we like the notion of better (fitter) things winning out over weaker things. It gives us a flattering (and strictly unDarwinian) sense of an underlying direction, a natural progression supposedly inherent in the mechanics of evolution and thus by implication of the justness of our place at the top of the pile. It also helps us post-hoc: it helps us post-rationalize the qualities in the thing or the person that has won out in some version of 'life's struggle'.

1. Geospiza magnirostris.
2. Geospiza fortis.
3. Geospiza parvula.
4. Certhidea olivacea.

Darwin's finches
Source: http://en.wikipedia.org/wiki/File:Darwin%27s_finches_by_Gould.jpg

When someone asks, 'why did Susan Boyle wind up being so successful in *Britain's Got Talent* Series 3?' (and ultimately become one of the world's leading recording artists), 'because she was the best' or 'because she had a surprising combination of voice and face' both seem much more comfortable answers than 'because she got lucky' or 'that's just the way things turned out' – it reinforces our sense that the world is ordered and that quality should out.

However, before and above 'fitness' and 'selection', Darwin's model of evolution relies fundamentally on two other things: the transmission of traits from generation to generation and the means of introducing variations in those traits over variations.

Both of these are delivered by copying – without copying, no transmission and no variation. And without these everything would stay the same – perhaps as the hard core creationists suggest, with each species just as they started. None of the variation that, for example, Darwin observed in the shape of closely related finches would have occurred. None of the stuff that happens generation by generation.

COPYING, CHANGING AND PERIOD INSTRUMENTS

The importance of copying in creating value this way is particularly clear in those arts in which the output is not one single, fixed thing: in the theatre, each production and each performance of a play introduces some variation – intended or otherwise – which is why many theatre actors enjoy long-run productions that allow them to evolve and develop their performances over time.

Similarly, each performance of a song changes the arrangement slightly, sometimes in ways that get picked up and repeated, sometimes just in temporary 'variations'.

Each telling of a joke changes that joke in the same way, each recounting of an anecdote subtly (and sometimes less subtly) twists the facts and the detail of that anecdote.

Sometimes this is more akin to the monkeys and typewriter story – much of what is produced is just noise – but now and again and more often if the players or comedians are good, something great happens.

Compare this, if you will, with those forms of creative activity which involve building a specific and static thing (or those who'd rather freeze the play or story or its telling in its original form). Variation and copying is far more problematic here, whether it is Shakespeare not done in Elizabethan dress (as my father would prefer) or classical music played with period instruments. While these kinds of artistic archaeology projects are interesting and can add real insight to our appreciation of a historical artwork, they are far from the whole story.

> ## " Copying brings change if you let it. "

Copying brings change if you let it – particularly if you let humans get involved and do their thing (which is approximate rather than precise). And in creative matters, copying is legend.

What follows are some more practical ways in which you can make copying work to create novelty and variation: fixing things, copying from far away and iteration.

COPYING AND FIXING THINGS

One way of deploying copying as the core mechanic of innovation is focusing on 'fixing' things that are broken.

While you may have learned at high school that Scottish engineer James Watt was the Father of the Industrial Revolution, being the *inventor* of the steam engine, the truth is rather different.[36]

❝ Focus on 'fixing' things that are broken. ❞

Thomas Newcomen was one of several individuals in the early part of the 18th Century who worked on steam engines to pump water more than 150 feet out of the deep Cornish tin mines to make deeper geological seams accessible.

Newcomen's engine was based – like others of the day – on steam and vacuum. It worked remarkably well in that it claimed to replace the strength of 500 horses used in previous machines (hence horsepower), but it had some obvious weaknesses that Watt identified.

Above all, it was energy inefficient: it required the cylinder to be alternatively heated by steam (most of which was lost as the cylinder cooled to working pressure) and then cooled by jets of cold water.

❝ Watt didn't 'invent' anything, he innovated on Newcomen's design. ❞

Watt's breakthrough design was a 'fix' to Newcomen's engine: specifically he improved what he'd inherited by adding an external condenser for the steam which drove the pistons so that the main cylinder didn't have to cool and be heated repeatedly (and thus lose a lot of the energy created).

In addition, he subsequently switched the beams which the engine drove to rotary ones, but the heart of Watt's innovation was what you might now call a 'hack' rather than an innovation.

Contrary to what we've been told by the textbooks, Watt didn't 'invent' anything, he innovated on Newcomen's design. He fixed by copying. Good copying, that is.

For 20 years, he and his partner, Matthew Bolton, vigorously defended their patent rights against further improvements by users. Their business model – one based on leasing rather than ownership – was a great deal of help in keeping users from both doing their own hacks on the Watt-Newcomen design and from sharing these hacks with each other. But their support in the legal profession was particularly advantageous.

Watt became grumpier – like a Dickensian villain, cowering in the shadows of his residence, plotting his revenge – and lost many friends by clinging on so tightly to the legal protection to his IP. By the time his patent rights eventually lapsed (at the turn of the 19th Century), he was extremely rich but alone and embittered. Thereafter, he failed to make another sale. Why would anyone buy from him, when they could learn from each other even better solutions? The descriptively named 'Lean's Engine Reporter' which then appeared was one of several platforms which appeared in order to provide the platform for many of the engineering community to share 'fixes' and 'hacks'. Which in turn provided similar scales of improvement in productivity that Watt had originally achieved, albeit compared to Watt's product rather than Newcomen's. The great 'fix' of the one-time University instrument maker was now common-knowledge and therefore effectively worthless.[37]

FIXING BROKEN THINGS

Fixing broken things is a more proactive approach to helping copying work and one which I've used repeatedly in helping clients innovate new services and products.

First, you identify what's broken for users in a particular service, say in a particular market like household insurance. Then you set about solving that as best you can, as simply as you can. Most of the original product or service abides – it's been copied across – but you've 'fixed' the 'broken' bit.

> ❝ **Most of the original product or service abides, but you've 'fixed' the 'broken' bit.** ❞

If this sounds familiar, this is because it has become a commonly used grammar in start-up pitches, not only to communicate to potential investors the idea at the heart of the start-up, but also to root the product or service in what customers really need: *X is broken, we will fix it by…Y.*

Can I just make one request: can we please stop trying to 'fix' things that aren't broken? Or, at least, focus on what's broken for the customer…*really*.

I recently heard a pitch for a product that aimed 'fix' Karaoke. Now there are things that ARE broken here (for example the font-size of the catalogues often make it hard to make a choice late at night in a darkened bar, but not being fun is not one of things that Karaoke lacks. For most of us, anyway.

POPULAR THING FOR A BROKEN THING

John V. Willshire has a great game to do this more directly – copying both broken thing and its solution. He calls it 'Popular thing for a broken thing':

- First, encourage individual players to identify a number of things that don't work for consumers or users of a particular category. Each player should write down two of these that seem most pressing and urgent from the users' perspective. These then get pooled for the team to use.
- Second, individuals are encouraged to identify two services (on- or offline) in any other category[38] which they particularly like and which they think others could learn from. Again these get written on separate cards and pooled for the team's resource.
- Now the team is encouraged to create 'popular' solutions for 'broken things' by assembling appropriate pairs of both sorts of thing, broken and popular.

The remarkable thing about this game is that it rarely disappoints: the result is always several great hitherto unimagined solutions to real problems that the business has habitually ignored (because they seem too hard).

BROKEN THINGS AT SCALE

In one large scale version of this (at Insight Innovation Exchange Amsterdam in Winter 2014), my colleagues and I first asked the hundreds of market research buyers and sellers to identify the broken things in their market and then together, under our guidance, to fix them by stealing from elsewhere.

My favourite hack here was the one created with Mike Macleod of Atlanta, GA.

PROBLEM: Nobody wins from current big company procurement rules:

- Small vendors can't afford to go through the tendering process and struggle with the paperwork and financial pain of procurement-led contracts.
- Large buyers don't get what they really want – they find hard to make occasional use of the boutique suppliers.
- Large vendors can do the procurement procedure (clearly some are better than others) and are really good at managing their costs at scale but cannot afford to have the boutique mentality on their staff line.

SOLUTION: Steal the model from the aerospace industry:

- Create 1st and 2nd tier contractors.
- 1st tier contractors can act (at least part of the time) as 'talent agents' to bring corporate buyers and boutique vendors together.
- 1st tier contractors can manage logistics and finances without having to buy the boutique or carry their overhead.

Thus far this chapter has shown how copying can create novelty and become the engine for innovation if we follow certain conditions:

- Copy loosely.
- Encourage error/variation by repeated copying.
- Focus on fixing broken things (and by copying over what's not broken).

But there's another essential way to use copying to innovate: *copying from far away*.

SUMMARY SO FAR

VERY SMALL OR FAR AWAY?

The cult TV show *Father Ted* celebrated the craziness of a home for wayward Catholic priests on the self-explanatory Craggy Island. Our favourite episode features the marvellous spectacle of the self-important Father Ted sitting in a rain-swept caravan, explaining the notion of perspective to the dim-witted Father Dugal by comparing a toy cow in his hand with a real one outside in the field. 'OK, one last time. These are small … but the ones out there are far away. Small … far away … !'[39] he intones, with increasing frustration.

Here's the thing: copying from far away is valuable because it's likely to be loose. It can't help but bring error, variation and a new perspective to an issue. This is how it creates novelty and innovation.

One version of this is what's known as 'mash-up' culture: where two previously unconnected bits of content get mashed together to make something new. Hip-hop and other similar musical genres are often rooted in the collision of previously unconnected things. Aerosmith and Run DMC's *Walk This Way* being perhaps the earliest example that crossed over into the mainstream.

"Copying from far away is likely to be loose."

Today's music recording and editing technology make these things much easier but the practice still thrives in music (despite the long arm of the copyright lawyers). Perhaps the finest example of this is DJ/producer Danger Mouse's *Grey Album*, a haunting concoction of acapella tracks from JayZ's *The Black Album* and music and sounds from the Beatles' *White Album*.

Another version – again musical – is clear in the self-explanatory game played week after week on BBC Radio Four's long running 'antidote to panel games' *Sorry I Haven't A Clue*, 'One Song to the Tune of Another'.[40] As the name of the game suggests, contestants are invited to sing the words of one song to the melody of another. Some of my favourite examples include comedian Graeme Garden singing the words of *Kung Fu Fighting* to the tune of *Greensleeves*, *Hit Me with your Rhythm Stick* to the music of *O Sole mio* or *Blame it on the Boogie* to the melody of the *Battle Hymn of the Republic*. Of course, these unimagined collisions are funny because they are absurd, but also because they open up new perspectives on both music and lyrics. New coming from old, again.

Of course, the art of mash-up is taking two unrelated things and putting them together and creating serendipitous novelty from the combination. But stealing from a distance has a much longer and more respectful tradition in the arts.

OVER THERE, OVER THERE …

The great modernist poet, critic and literary editor, TS Eliot, put a great deal of value not on whether a poet copies – like most artists he acknowledged the central role that copying, borrowing and creative response to art all play in their creative process – but on *how he or she copies*. And how far away their source material is.

> 'A good poet' Eliot observes[41] 'will usually borrow from authors remote in time, or alien in language, or diverse in interest.'

Great artists take enormous pride in copying from a distance: Picasso was at different times obsessed with African masks and Ancient Greek ceramics as he looked to develop new ways of representing human forms and different ways of seeing.

But in many other fields, successful innovation is dependent on copying from far away.

THE MAKING OF MODERN RUSSIA

More than any other individual, Tsar Peter the Great is responsible for the creation of Modern Russia and its institutions (many of which laid the ground for and survived the 1917 Revolution): for its transformation from a medieval state, dominated by an all-seeing Church, a backward and inward looking nobility and a society structured around a very feudal serfdom in which most individuals belonged to those whose land they worked and whose coffers they filled.

Thanks to his enlightened tutors, Peter had developed a profound interest in the modern world – in the great post-medieval societies and their practices beyond the borders of the ancient Russian Lands – and sought to open Russia up to this world. So it was, in 1697, that he set off on what has become known as the Grand Embassy – a tour of Western Europe whose primary goals were only partly fulfilled – the strengthening of the pan-European alliance against the Ottoman Empire and the creation of a Western alliance against the Swedish crown. But his secondary goal – of learning more of the practices that made the modern world what it is – was far more successful.

He brought back (German) fashions (he was particularly known for his dislike of the beards that dominated Russian

style at the time and banned the nobility from wearing them) and English social rituals (tea drinking, for example).

" All of these innovations were borrowed, copied and stolen. "

Like some 17th-Century gap-year student, he dragged back know-how and expertise from each of the countries he visited: he had long been particularly keen on shipbuilding and sailing (even though when he came to the throne, Russia only had a single maritime port at Arkhangelsk on the White Sea). During the Grand Embassy, he managed to secure four months of anonymous but hands-on experience in the shipyards of the Dutch East India Company and conducted visits to Deptford and Greenwich under the patronage of William III (then ruler of Britain and the Netherlands).

He also learned much from the Dutch engineers about engineering and draining marshland and from the British about city building (his visit to Manchester seems a particularly memorable one to modern minds!) – knowledge, expertise and contacts which he subsequently put to work in the construction of his dream city, St Petersburg.

He also reformed the governance of Russian clergy along Western lines (though letting them keep their beards) and perhaps most strikingly the official calendar, shifting it to

the Julian Calendar (calculated from the birth of Christ rather than the Creation) and in doing so moved the official start of the year from 1 September to 1 January.

All of these innovations were Peter's for sure; but all of them borrowed, copied and stolen from what he saw during his travels.

LET THE DOGS OUT

When Swiss electrical engineer Georges de Mestral returned one evening in 1948 from a hunting trip in the Alpine forest above his home in Commugny in the Vaudois, he discovered his dog's fur (and his own socks and breaches) were covered with burdock burrs (those sticky seed heads that seem to stick to everything).

Being a curious so-and-so, de Mestral decided to put the pesky things under his microscope and was fascinated to discover the curious micro-hook and loop system that underpins the stickiness of burrs – on man, dog and textiles.

Perhaps, he pondered, this might provide some alternative to the zipper – then the gold-standard non-button fastener.

To start with few of the people Mestral talked to took his idea seriously, but during a trip to Lyon (then one of

Europe's leading centres of cotton weaving) he started to explore how to make it workable. While cotton prototypes showed some initial promise, they wore out very quickly and it was only when he turned to the more robust nylon that the idea became worthwhile.

Today, few remember de Mestral but all of us know Velcro – that highly effective fastening system for apparel based on understanding how the distinctive seedpod of certain plants spreads itself far and wide. Most people imagine that his first major client (NASA) must have 'invented' the technology, whereas the truth is de Mestral copied from nature.

Copying from nature – 'biomimicry' as biologist Janine Benyus and her colleagues call it – comes in all shapes and sizes. It can – like Mestral's work – merely involve copying a mechanism that evolution has developed for one purpose to solve a problem in another.

A striking example is the (shinkansen) Japanese bullet train's 15-metre-long nose which helps the train go faster and reduces 'tunnel boom' (huge sonic disruptions caused by air compression): this design is based on the extended bill of the kingfisher which minimizes air and water resistance and turbulence as the bird dives for its food.

"Copying from nature – biomimicry – comes in all shapes and sizes."

Similarly, the pharmaceutical industry has long been aware of how plants and animals might offer new chemical breakthroughs to modern medicine: while the medicine of the ancient Egyptians used products of the willow tree (gen. Salix) in pain relief, it wasn't until 1853 that the French chemist Charles Frédéric Gerhardt synthesized acetylsalicylic acid (ASA), or 'aspirin' as we know it, as a copy of the active ingredient. No wonder they scour the world for 'native' medicine practices of indigenous people as the start point for their own work.

Biomimicry can also involve more metaphorical copying. For example, our notion of a business 'ecosystem' really helps uncover new insights for businesses struggling to understand a complex and rapidly changing world. Equally, as discussed earlier in this chapter, the biologically-derived theory of evolution can provide real insights into how technology develops or how behaviours change as they get adopted by more and more people. Phase transitions or fluid mechanics can provide huge insights into the behaviour of large crowds or populations of human agents.

Biomimicry, too, is based on copying – copying from far away.

THE BRAINJUICER® EFFECT

Bright-eyed and mischievous, John Kearon started BrainJuicer® PLC in 1999 with the hunch that the rather staid and mature market research world was ripe for innovation. Today his company is a multi-million dollar business with offices in five continents and a reputation of being the most innovative company in its sector.

How did he manage this? While existing players busied themselves with improving on existing practices with marginal gains on industry performance, Kearon looked elsewhere – far away to emerging insights from social science.

When I first knew him, Kearon was fascinated with the wisdom of crowds phenomenon: how, under the right circumstances, the cognitive power of the crowd can be greater than the smartest (or best informed) individual or expert.

Kearon and his colleagues found ways of prototyping and testing different ways of making the 'wisdom of crowds work'. They examined the academic online models of the Iowa Electronic Markets (large scale online platforms which are a mix between futures trading environments and betting shops) and smaller simpler models, before developing their own approach which uses the basic insight that in order for the crowd to be wise, individuals have to act independently (otherwise our friend copying will lead to the kind of 'herding' effects that denote booms and busts in real world financial markets).

Similarly, Kearon applied the work of psychologist Paul Ekman on the facial 'ticks' and 'tells' that reveal our emotional response to stimuli to market research, not to read the faces of consumers as you might imagine but to help them to answer questions about their own emotions. It's far easier to point to one of eight faces to say how you feel than find the words.

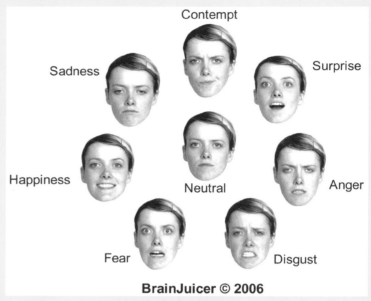

BrainJuicer © 2006

FaceTrace® reproduced with permission of BrainJuicer Group, PLC

BOTTLING THE JUICER'S RECIPE

It's worth pulling out the essential recipe for 'Juicy' innovation:

- First, seek out a problem to solve – a real problem or shortfall in customer satisfaction. Something that doesn't work for your customer.
- Second, find a distant skillset or perspective that you feel might help.
- Third, make a prototype rapidly (do this cheaply because it won't work first time) and get real world feedback on your idea as soon and as often as you can.

RINSE AND REPEAT

If Kearon copies from afar, he also keeps copying the copy he has made. So even if something he's stolen seems to work pretty quickly in the new context, he keeps copying the prototype and creating error: 'It's important to break things – that's the only way to know what the real mechanics are and their real limits.'

I call that 'rinse and repeat'.

All creative people do it. The very visual example of Matisse's bronzes described earlier is echoed in the exhibit that award-winning American architect Frank Gehry produced for the Biennale: in it, he showed the evolution of his design for the LA Opera House he designed through the 100 or so sketches and models he made. Each one was an iteration of the previous design and each one slightly different.

Whatever you've stolen, copy it again and again. See if you can evolve it through copying it loosely, any which way you can.

My good friend, cartoonist Hugh 'gapingvoid' Macleod sees this as an important part of his working method, too. As he works, the 'definitive' version emerges. So, too with the products and services he's developed around this content. As he puts it:

Copy, copy, copy.

Reproduced with permission of Gapingvoid Art

STEALING FROM A DISTANCE – GAMES TO PLAY

There are a number of ways in which you can bring stealing from a distance alive in your strategizing that don't involve a lengthy study of the darker corners of cognitive science.

In his best-seller, *Eat Big Fish*, Adam Morgan highlights the approach of Ian Shraeger. You may not know the name but you certainly know his finest work – the boutique hotel concept. Shraeger was one of the entrepreneurs behind the 1970s NYC nightclub, Studio 54.

After a brief sojourn in jail for tax offences (telling journos that the only business in Manhattan making more money than you is the mafia is a strategy you might choose not to copy – it's the kind of thing that brings the Revenue running) and some time running an even glitzier nightclub, the Palladium, with huge state of the art video screens and collaborations with New York's leading designers and architects, Shraeger and partner Bill Lavell turned their attention to a business they knew nothing about: hotels.

Now around this time, the 1980s, the hotel industry both in Manhattan and elsewhere was stultified – décor and architecture were at best 'high Jewish Baroque' and at worst, tired and overpriced Holiday Inns. Shraeger and team brought the sensibility of the nightclub to the market: rather than a small lobby leading to larger private spaces (the accommodation), they created huge public areas – at Morgans, The Royalton and the Paramount – and tiny, dark bedrooms (who needs to sleep?). Style, celebrity and, yes, glitter. The 'boutique' hotel concept was born.

Porting the rules of one market to a new one often reveals unforeseen opportunity and fresh insights like this. The further away the better.

> **Porting the rules of one market to another often reveals fresh insight.**

Knowing how things should be done – what the rules are – in any context can often be a handicap. Not knowing about the 'should' can create real opportunities (so long as you bring your assumptions and new rules from a long way away). This is why innovation is often a liminal activity – those who don't really know what they're supposed to do or don't fully understand the rules.

WHAT WOULD THE DUDE DO?

Our version of this is a game based on the 'Dude', the iconic character in *The Big Lebowski*, played by Jeff Bridges.

Asking what the Dude would do in these circumstances is the stepping off point for copying rules from a distant market or context (for those of you who haven't seen the movie, the Dude is a remarkable Californian drop-out who bowls and drinks white Russians all day and all night until he finds himself entangled in a noir-ish plot).

Why focus on a person? Well, we humans are very good at people thinking – better often than we are at things or abstract ideas.

A line of contemporary social science research which examines how stories change as they spread – transmission chain studies – serves to demonstrate this. What people seem to remember is the people stuff not the technical stuff; what's more, contrary to what the evolutionary psychologists have suggested it's not the stuff of obvious evolutionary advantage – just the people stuff.

No wonder most people find it so easy to think about something afresh by borrowing the persona or someone else – a famous leader or a brand. *Like the Dude …*

It's like putting on a mask. What would you do if you were …?

Here are some simple examples:

- What would Apple do to furniture retailing?
- What would a Leninist cell phone business look like?
- What would the Murdochs do to the health sector (perhaps it'd be better not to ask …)?
- What would Facebook do to the vacation business?
- What would JayZ do to the automotive business?
- What would Paul Smith do to the music business?
- What would Batman do to the energy market?

Write down the things you think this person or business would do (try not to worry about the impracticality).

Debrand it and ask yourself what you are left with. What can you steal? In the 'what' and the 'how' of the answers.

NOT BEING ME

A large part of the value from doing exercises like this comes from the way the external persona/brand liberates you from your assumptions about what is and what isn't acceptable.

I run a brains-trust format for clients which seeks to do this on a larger scale: if, for example, the central challenge is about changing health behaviour in UK offices, I will pool a brains trust of diverse experts, including in this case an anthropologist, a social psychologist, an expert in behaviour change programmes in the developing world and of course an architect who specializes in designing spaces which encourage the productive interaction of people.

" It is tempting to look too closely. "

Each expert is asked to review their experience and the literature in their discipline and share perspectives and indicated action. So while the anthropologist might not have much to say about the office context, he or she does have a lot to say about behaviour change around health in other contexts. By contrast, the architect has an extraordinary perspective on the nature of the office environment and understanding interaction and behaviour change within it.

The point here is this: very often it is tempting look *too closely* at the phenomena you are trying to study. You can get blinded by detail and by the assumptions you make about how a thing works and how to influence it. Borrowing the knowledge of other disciplines and other experiences can provide a liberating new perspective as well as rapid 'hacks'.

LEAVE YOUR JOB

Equally, metaphorically leaving your job – as the management team at Motorola famously did to transform themselves into a cell-phone business – can create the cognitive space to imagine things that are unimaginable inside the business with its default unspoken assumptions about how things work.

I often encourage this kind of mental exercise with my clients in thinking about themselves as 'founders' of a start-up, freed from the unspoken but weighty needs of the corporation, its past and its cultural assumptions. Anything is up for grabs then.

Compare and contrast the marketer who seeks 'sector experience' as a priority from his advisors and suppliers – if you only know exactly what everyone else you know knows, how can you innovate? Know more or less or – more importantly – different.

KNOWING WHAT TO COPY

Part of the value of copying as an innovation tool lies in whom and what we copy. As evolutionary economist, Sam Bowles, has suggested: knowing who or what to copy is essential to our species' success. So it is with the organizations that employ us.

So if everybody copied Richard Branson – or Donald Trump – we'd clearly not all be successful. Actually, it's a frightening thought to imagine an army of blond Bransons or flammably flame-haired Trumps. And in any case, would the excess of Branson-rebels all counter each other out?

" Part of the value must come from scarcity or absence. "

So part of the value of copying must lie in the scarcity value of what or whom we copy. If we all copy the same people then we'd end up with a similar outcome to single white copying (described earlier) and that's not at all what we want.

Instead, let's consider two other dimensions: success and relevance.

" Copying success is as old as the hills. "

Religions tend to encourage their adherents to follow the example of an ideal individual: in the Christian traditions, Imitatio Christi (the imitation of Christ) is a recurring motif.

From the early Church fathers like St Augustine who viewed it as an essential remedy to the sins of Adam to the extreme versions both within and without the late medieval Catholic Church – on the one hand, St Francis of Assisi who insisted on following both the physical and spiritual example of Jesus (hence his vow of poverty); on the other, the early protestant theologians who sought to find their own fresh alternative to the Catholic establishment's smoke, bells and papery – copying the example of the biblical Jesus has long been held as a way to a successful life. All religions use stories and examplars to encourage successful living (as they define it).

The fairy stories and folk tales we have always told each other (but more importantly told our children) contain similar injunctions (beware the forest, beware the unknown,

beware greed). As novelist, critic and fairy story expert Marina Warner puts it:

'Fairy tales are about money, marriage, and men. They are the maps and manuals that are passed down from mothers and grandmothers to help them survive.'

HOW TO WIN FRIENDS

In the modern era we love copying success: Dale Carnegie's *How to Win Friends and Influence People* was the first major self-help best-seller, selling some 15 million copies around the world since publication in 1936.

Fifty years later, Steven Covey's *7 Habits of Highly Effective People* did much the same on an even grander scale – more than 25 million copies in any number of different languages have been bought.

Why? Because this kind of book gives a blueprint for how successful individuals behave that anyone can emulate and thus (theoretically, at least) become successful, too.

Since Covey's success there have been a flurry of 'Habits' books in different spheres – whatever insight they might contain and whatever empirical research they are based on, they remain simple rule-based descriptions of success. Not just the great *Built to Last: Successful Habits of Visionary Companies* but the more mundane *25 Sales Habits of Successful Salespeople*, and the gender specific *Successful Women Think Differently: 9 Habits to Make you Happier, Healthier, and More Resilient* or the obviously derivative *7 Habits of Successful Slimmers*.

❝ Copying success is still a great default choice. ❞

The arrival of the internet, blogging and social media have just amplified this tendency – the 'listification' of success – further. 'Ten secrets about the future of content creation', 'The 5 rules of making your video viral', '20 ways to drive traffic to your blog' are all great 'link bait' post headlines.

Try it yourself: pop 'habits of successful' into Google along with a profession, skill or hobby and see how many blog posts and articles come up. Copying success is a great default.

THE CASE OF THE CASE STUDY

Nowadays, the 'case study' format is ubiquitous in business books and in business conversations. This seems part of this same trend.

The use of a case study works so well not just because it's a great storytelling device (we all use examples to build our case, from Malcolm Gladwell to our own work here), nor just because it seems 'scientific' (case studies are marvellous for illustrating principles or providing memorable anchors for the same or to bring a highly conceptual phenomenon alive but they are terrible for the business of doing empirical science – case studies focus on the individual instance not the generalized learnings from multiple cases).

No, case studies work and continue to be popular because they also provide a template for copying. *Why don't we do what so and so did? Why don't we just copy that?* This is what most people mean by 'case study'.

But how in this modern world – with so much choice and so much to sift through – can we identify authentic success? How can we tell the spurious and the snake-oil from the reliably successful?

One way of answering this is to check over the longer term:

- Which strategies are merely associated with success and which causally connected?
- Which always bring success and which only sometimes do?
- Which solve which kinds of problem? What is each suitable for?

THE RIGHT TOOL FOR THE RIGHT JOB

There are those who are organized and those who are not. My fishing buddy Jon is the former and I am the latter. Jon's tackle bag is neat, organized and free of extraneous line, hooks or gadgetry and it stays this way during our long days at the lakeside. My bag by contrast is a mess – so much so that I can sense Jon's discomfort and rising anxiety as he approaches to borrow some item or other, both of us knowing full well that we will have to reveal the tangle inside!

Equally, my household toolkit (with hammers, drills and the like) is distributed around our house in a fairly ad-hoc manner but my father-in-law's is hung neatly on the wall, sorted by size and function, each tool on an appropriate hook – it's not that he has outlines painted on the wall for each tool but it is disconcertingly tidy to my way of thinking.

Personal style aside, there is something to be said for the more organized approach It's easier to find what you're looking for: to find the right tool for the job, not just the nearest one – or your favourite one.

Of course, if you need a nail banging in to a floorboard, then you reach straight for the hammers. But is that really what you need?

66 What's needed is an easier-to-use resource. 99

THE VIRTUE OF A TIDY TOOLKIT

This is true of behaviour change and marketing strategy too: despite the incredible value created for us by behavioural economists in the last few years, the toolkit is unwieldy. Not just the huge collections of 'cognitive biases' – those ticks and quirks of human cognition that explain why we each of us do the odd things we do – that constitute the formal literature in this space. Our friend Rory Sutherland was wont to wave one such volume describing 140 different biases until others were discovered (and his arm started to ache).

Of course you can use these or similar strategic resources if you're prepared to put in the hard yards, but we've found very few behaviour change or marketing strategists and even fewer generalists who are prepared to make the effort.

What's needed is an easier-to-use resource: a compendium of examples of successful strategies sorted in a simpler way, according to the kind of behaviour that they're trying to change.

A 'KINDA THING' KIND OF THING

I wrote in the Introduction of the *tyranny of the singular*: our tendency to treat every situation as unique and singular and thus requiring not just huge skill and expertise but a singular solution.

Now this might be very flattering for the problem owner ('no-one before has faced a problem quite as difficult as this so if you overcome it, you will be first among men' etc.) and indeed, very flattering for the strategic knight errant ('only the very brightest and best could possibly solve this conundrum') but it is rarely true.

And even if it is true, it's not very helpful to assume that it is. It makes the problem seem really hard or indeed impossible.

The truth is that most things are like other things – certainly they seem that way: the human mind's ability to see similarities and connections between things is unbounded.

Hence the importance of metaphor and simile in human thinking and communication.

KINDA THING

No, this 'kinda' thing is very human.

The amazing animal behaviour expert, writer and autist, Temple Grandin has written eloquently about what how animals and autistic individuals (on the one hand) and neuro-normals (the rest of us) perceive the world – they see every detail, our brains sort the detail before it leaves the occipital zones. They see a piece of foil flashing in the sunlight and go on seeing it, we see it flashing, interpret it as a something like a piece of foil and dismiss it. A piece of flashing foil kinda thing.

The neuroscientist Antonio Damasio, whose work (e.g. *Descartes' Error*[42]) popularized many of the contemporary insights into how brains work, makes a similar point when he describes the difference between the responses of two proto humans, who walking through the forest see what looks like a snake.

The one with the 'kinda' facility is the one who runs and lives to fight/hunt another day; the one without it has to investigate, gets bitten and dies.

Approximate is in many ways more useful than precise. 'Kinda?' more than 'how much?'

So what the next chapter holds is an exploration of our simple sorting map to help you work out what kind of thing you are dealing with, before letting loose on the strategy archives (the What To Copy bit, proper).

CONCLUSION

Copying can keep things the same (Bad Copying)

Or, it can change things, creating new and different ideas (Good Copying)

Good Copying delights in error and variation – this is where the juice is, not in replication

Good Copying is loose rather than tight

Good Copying looks far away rather than nearby

Good Copying delights in rinse and repeat

Good Copying seeks to fix broken things

And finally, Good Copying asks different kinds of ("kinda") questions

> **" I have always liked drawing: when you draw you see more intensely. "**
> —Henry Moore

What this chapter will cover:

Knowing what kind of problem you've got is an essential step in working out from where you should be copying – what kind of thing is appropriate to copy.

So, this chapter will explore a way of drawing and mapping behaviours against one another which really helps you nail these 'what kinda?' questions.

This approach is based on the map my colleague Professor Alex Bentley and I developed back in 2007 and which we

described in a number of articles and in 2011's *I'll Have What She's Having.*

The important thing, here, is for you to learn to draw the map yourself, and by drawing think about 'what kind of thing' you're wrestling with – 'what kinda thing' you're trying to change.

So, to start with, here are some thoughts on drawing and thinking.

Get yourself a pen and some paper* and we'll begin.

*Or even some of John's fabulous Artefact Cards.

3

'WHAT KINDA THING?': MAPS AND DRAWING

What kind of thing are you trying to change?

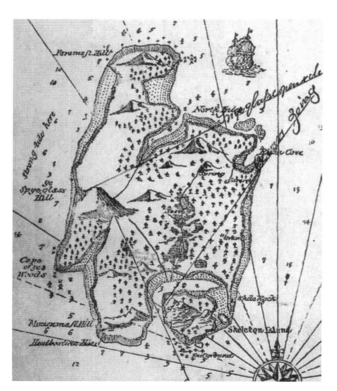

Stevenson's original map

Source: http://upload.wikimedia.org/wikipedia/commons/c/c6/Treasure-island-map.jpg

DRAWING IS THINKING

One afternoon in the wet summer of 1880, the newly married Robert Louis Stevenson started sketching a map of a make-believe island to amuse himself and his stepson. Those few strokes of the pen were to transform his professional life and reputation.

> 'As I pored upon my map of "Treasure Island" the future characters of my book began to appear there visibly among imagined woods; and their brown faces and bright weapons peered out to me from unexpected quarters, as they passed to and fro, fighting and hunting treasure on these very few square inches of a flat projection.'[43]

By drawing in the coves and the hilltops and the rivers and streams, the island came alive in his mind; very quickly the chapters of the classic pirate tale took shape – a children's story which has gone on to shape so much of our modern notions of pirates and piracy, of the looks, the rituals and the characters of that world. Stevenson fell to his task like a man possessed, writing a chapter every day and reading it to his captive audiences by night so that soon enough 'The Ship's Cook' (as he called the tale of Long John Silver) was ready for publication. Of course, we know the book better by the name he gave the island that emerged from that map he drew on paper – *Treasure Island*.

DUCO ERGO SUM[44]

Maps and map-making have long enjoyed a profound relationship with creative writing and storytelling. From the ancient travellers who would use maps as narrative frames, to tell and retell the stories of their voyages to the modern writers of fiction who create whole new worlds. Those twin fathers of English fantasy fiction, JRR Tolkien and CS Lewis, had both fiddled and doodled with their own fantasy maps since boyhood (in exactly the same way Stevenson and his stepson did that rainy afternoon). Interestingly both responded creatively to the incredible illustrator Pauline Baynes who drew the maps that illustrated their early editions; the work of both the writer and illustrator intermingling over time so that both admitted they started to see their lands and peoples through the eyes of the illustrator.

"Drawing helps us see connections between things."

Making visual representations of things and ideas and their interrelationships can provide us with the means to see the connections between things in the real world – not just in time and space. Psychologist Steven Pinker suggests this is peculiarly human.

'Cognitive psychology has shown that the mind best understands facts when they are woven into a conceptual fabric, such as a narrative, mental map, or intuitive theory. Disconnected facts in the mind are like unlinked pages on the Web: they might as well not exist.'[45]

Things not drawn 'might as well not exist' is an interesting insight: both in the sense that the thoughts and ideas you don't write down and/or draw just drift away and disappear from sight. Somehow without being made tangible they never quite land.

Cartoonist Robert Crumb puts it this way: 'Drawing is a way for me to articulate things inside myself that I can't otherwise grasp.'

" Until you've drawn your idea you haven't really thought it through. "

Similarly, John V Willshire (who invented the cards on which I built this book and did many of the illustrations that run through the book) insists, 'until you've drawn your idea to show it to somebody else, you haven't really thought it through'. My colleagues and I make our clients do this a lot. A lot.

Richard Sennett makes the same point about the tangible nature of 'drawing-thinking' in *The Craftsman* when he cites a young MIT architect saying:

> *'when you draw a site, when you put in the counter lines and the trees, it becomes ingrained in your mind. You come to know the site in a way that is not possible with the [CADCAM] computer... You get to know a terrain by tracing and retracing it, not by letting the computer "regenerate" it for you.'*[46]

The brilliant Texan writer and artist Austin Kleon (who shot to fame with his manifesto *Steal Like an Artist*[47]) puts this into practice in his workspace. He has two desks: one

analogue (with pens, pencils, ink, paint and paper) and the other digital (with laptop etc.). The former, he says, is where 'my work is born'; the latter where 'I edit, publish etc'.[48] One for thinking as making; the other to send it off to the world.

" It's worth assuming drawing IS thinking. "

Time and again in our work we come back to the truth of this – to the importance of drawing as a mode of thinking, rather than a complement to it, or an afterthought. Drawing and thinking are closely related. Indeed, in many important ways, it's worth assuming *drawing IS thinking*.

Let's be clear, by this I don't mean that you have to be an artist in order to think – far from it. It's just that drawing out the relationships between things forces you to think harder about them than you might do. Anyone can do it (this from the chap who was chucked out of art class at 14).

What follow are two historical examples of how drawing things made the thinking better, clearer and more impactful on those around the thinker – more practical and useful.

MAPPING SOHO

In the sweltering summer of 1854, London experienced its third major outbreak of cholera in the space of two decades. This time, in the space of just a few weeks, more than 10,000 died from a combination of crippling diarrhoea, vomiting and extreme dehydration. Today we think of cholera as primarily a disease of the developing world but in the first part of the 19th Century it spread rapidly from Bengal to Baltimore and everywhere in between, creating fear and terror as it did so. Not least because a century and a half ago, more often than not, cholera was fatal. In Russia alone, more than a million died of it between 1847 and 1851. Everywhere the condition spread – and the rapid rise of modern transport infrastructure gave it a lift wherever it wanted to go, from Asia to Europe and on to the New World – it killed tens of thousands, yet no-one seemed to know what to do about it.

It was a disease that lurked in the dark and dank and dangerous places and seemed to reach out of the shadows to drag off the young and the old suddenly and without warning, or so it seemed (these were after all the early days of modern epidemiology). The medical consensus at this time was that this kind of thing was an airborne infection – from 'bad' or 'night air' (hence also the Italian 'malaria'). 'Miasma' (from the Greek for 'pollution') was thought to be a vapour or mist full of particles of decomposing organic matter which caused various diseases including cholera and plague.

However, not everyone agreed with this. In London's Soho, Dr John Snow was particularly unconvinced. Working together with local clergyman Reverend Henry Whitehead he collated the data of all the cases of infection he could and plotted them on a map of the area around the Broad (now Broadwick) Street water pump.

'I found that nearly all the deaths had taken place within a short distance of the [Broad Street] pump. There were only ten deaths in houses situated decidedly nearer to another street-pump. In five of these cases the families of the deceased persons informed me that they always sent to the pump in Broad Street, as they preferred the water to that of the pumps which were nearer.... With regard to the deaths occurring in the locality belonging to the pump, there were 61 instances in which I was informed that the deceased persons used to drink the pump water from Broad Street, either constantly or occasionally... The result of the inquiry, then, is, that there was been no particular outbreak or prevalence of cholera in this part of London except among the persons who were in the habit of drinking the water of the above-mentioned pump well.'[49]

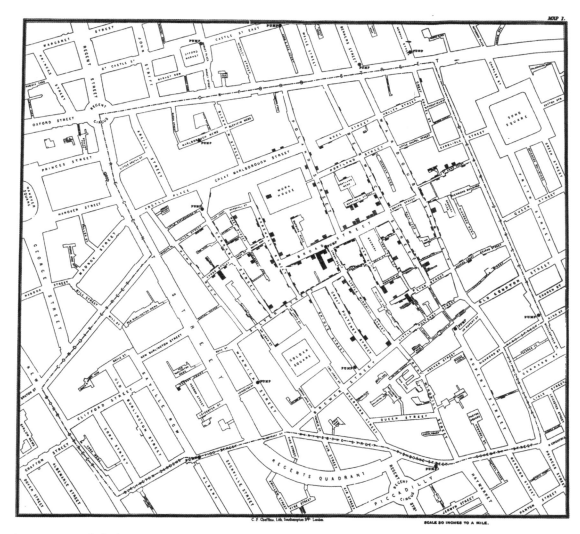

Snow's map of cholera cases

Source: http://en.wikipedia.org/wiki/John_Snow_(physician)

Most of us are unaware of the history that lies buried in the streets around us.

Few of the revellers who still gather together on fine Summer evenings on the pavement outside the John Snow public house (on what is now 'Broad', not Broadwick Street) have even noticed the old iron water pump which sits across from them; fewer still can tell the story of the life-saving work that focused on that metal curiosity and even fewer will appreciate the importance of Snow's detective work in saving millions of lives, even today in developing countries.*

Cholera, Snow established, was water-borne and not the product of 'bad air'.

Snow himself readily admitted the limits of his analysis – both on the specifics of the case (he failed to account for those leaving the area in his dataset) and the general (it would take many years for science to develop the microbiology that could finally squash the 'bad air' *miasma* theory.)

That said, his work had immediate impact – within 24 hours of the publication of Snow's report, the guilty pump was disabled by the Parish officials. And as it happened, subsequent excavation showed how right Snow had been in the specifics – inches away from the well, diggers discovered a leaking cess-pool, which had been secretly fouling the fresh drinking water. And his evidence-based approach provided a template for many others studying public health issues.

" Drawing things out like this can really help make clear what we might otherwise overlook. "

What's important for us here is that drawing things out like this can really help make clear what we might otherwise overlook – to help us see the otherwise invisible connections between things. Of course, there are other things that we might explore – nuances and specifics – but using a map to plot phenomena together helps make sense for your reader and anyone you might be trying to explain your ideas to.

*Some of the local beer drinkers might joke darkly about the dangers of drinking the water in Soho; few will know that one of the few groups to remain unaffected during the 1854 Cholera attack, was that of the monks of the local monastery who brewed (and consumed) their own beer. Fermentation it seems, killed the Cholera.

NURSE, NURSE!

Florence Nightingale was one the great icons of the Age of Empire, the 'Lady with the Lamp', the pale faced angel of the wards. She was also a direct and precise contemporary of Snow. She too made a similarly important contribution to medicine by drawing a striking visualization of the causes of death: this, as she suspected, far more than the succour and comfort she gave the wounded and dying as a nurse, was to be her great and lasting contribution to medicine.

On the outbreak of the Crimean War, the intrepid Florence had managed to get herself invited by the War Minister George Herbert to lead a team of 38 trained British nurses to alleviate things, despite her parents' wishes to the contrary. What she learned at the hospital in Scutari and how she communicated it to the authorities was to change military and medical practice forever.

Her report, 'Notes on Matters Affecting the Health, Efficiency and Hospital Administration of the British Army' published in 1858, was a fearless piece of analysis, which spared no-one's blushes in the military and medical establishment, her own included, given what it revealed about the hugely negative role hospitals and hospital care played in soldiers' recovery.

Technically speaking this is a *polar area diagram*: medical data from each of 12 months of a given year is plotted around the central pole. The greater the area of a particular piece, the greater the number of casualties. The brilliance of this simple diagram is that it also shows, within each month's casualty section, how many of those casualties are from wounds received in battle and how many from disease and other causes. At a glance it's clear that the Russians and their allies proved to be only a minor cause of death in these hospitals: the real enemy were diseases patients caught from each other – cholera, typhus and dysentery.

" Both use the map rather than the data to communicate. "

Nightingale's visual works because it makes the relationship between things clear and unambiguous to the reader; Snow's work – at a different scale of complexity – does precisely the same thing about a complex and poorly understood phenomenon. Both use data to drive the visuals and ensure their thinking is sound but use the map rather than the data per se to communicate their meaning.

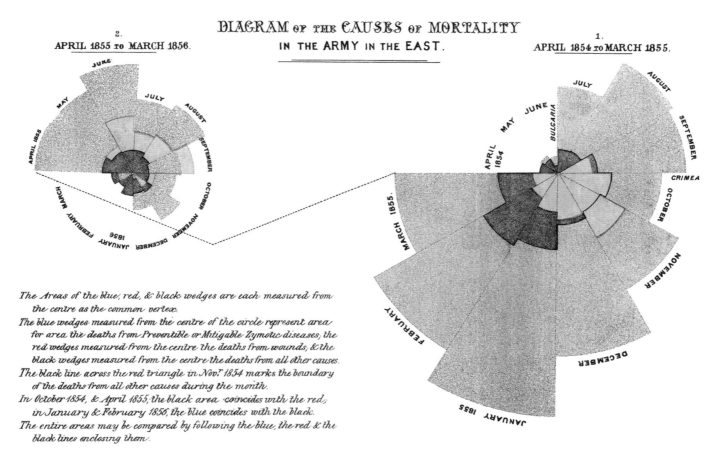

DIAGRAM OF THE CAUSES OF MORTALITY
IN THE ARMY IN THE EAST.

2.
APRIL 1855 TO MARCH 1856.

1.
APRIL 1854 TO MARCH 1855.

The Areas of the blue, red, & black wedges are each measured from the centre as the common vertex.

The blue wedges measured from the centre of the circle represent area for area the deaths from Preventible or Mitigable Zymotic diseases; the red wedges measured from the centre the deaths from wounds, & the black wedges measured from the centre the deaths from all other causes.

The black line across the red triangle in Nov.r 1854 marks the boundary of the deaths from all other causes during the month.

In October 1854, & April 1855, the black area coincides with the red; in January & February 1855, the blue coincides with the black.

The entire areas may be compared by following the blue, the red & the black lines enclosing them.

Causes of mortality in the army in the East

Source: http://commons.wikimedia.org/wiki/File:Nightingale-mortality.jpg

MEANWHILE BACK IN THE DEPARTMENT

Back in 2007, when Alex Bentley and I were trying to pull together our insights from the extensive analysis we were conducting on behalf of the UK Department of Health, we too resorted to creating a simple map of how people choose in order to show the relationships – the similarities and the differences – between different kinds of behaviour that patterns in the data revealed to us.

It's not a map which describes the behaviour of every individual at all times – it's not what marketers call a 'segmentation' which sorts out individuals in a population according to differences in their attitudes to a particular issue or category or according to their buying behaviour or wealth and so on.

" A map of different ways of choosing. "

No, this is a map of different ways of choosing – it sorts behaviour out based on what the predominant choice style is in a particular market or population at a particular time, based on the signature patterns found in behavioural datasets (see the following 'Four different choice styles' section). Of course, it is possible to describe behaviour at other levels and in more detail: the point being that this simple map helps the strategist ask some pretty big questions about 'what kinda thing' both rapidly and with confidence in equal measure.

Let's just create the basic structure and then you can start to explore each of the parts of the map and begin to make it useful.

Do it yourself

For this exercise you're going to need a pen and a piece of paper. (Or an Artefact Card, maybe.)

First, draw yourself an x-axis (from left to right) so:

This dimension of the map you're making represents the degree to which a choice (say, buying a new car) is shaped by independent decision making (by what goes on between an individual's ears, if you like) and to what extent that choice is shaped by the choices of others or their recommendation or some other social factor (by what goes on in the *space between people*).

Now's a good time to label the axes 'independent' and 'social', so:

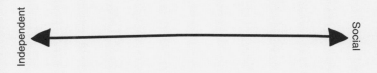

Many more things than we'd imagine are found on the social side of things – shaped by what goes on in the *space between people*. The names we give our children, the clothes we wear, the way we cut our hair, where we choose to live (this is

after all how cities grow), our ideas about attractiveness and fairness – even how we cast our votes in a democracy left to our own devices. Until recently, however, this has not been acknowledged: most of our models of human behaviour have focused primarily on the independent end of the scale – on what goes on between an individual's ears.[50]

As we'll see, many of our 'common sense' and even many of the new models of human behaviour downplay the importance of the social.

Now for the y-axis. Draw a vertical line down the page to cut the horizontal one in two. Label it 'informed' and 'uninformed' as shown in the 'Informed choice/uninformed choice' figure.

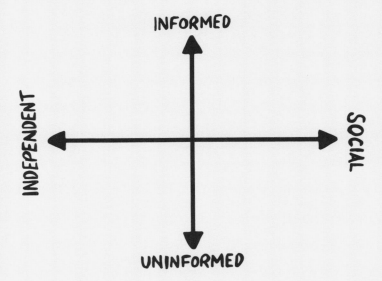

To understand this dimension, think for a moment of the stand-up comedian Eddie Izzard's routine about 'cake or death?'[51] In this skit, Izzard highlights that some choices in life are fairly easy because they are stark and binary (hence, 'cake or death?'). Until very recently, much of the thinking in economics and psychology dealt only with these kinds of decisions (and they are easy to research and model).

However, for most of us humans, most of the time, in what the social scientists call the 'decision landscape', the number of choices available to us is very different.

The average UK grocery store has more than 40,000 individual items (or 'SKUs') while the Walmart nearest to JFK airport in New York has nearer 100,000.

The music streaming service Spotify has more than 6 million pieces of music; iTunes store has more than 26 million.

The average European laptop market has more than 3,500 SKUs and there are thousands of household insurance products available each with many, many features to compare and contrast – so much so that companies have emerged who simply provide the means for you to compare these multi-faceted products and product options without you having to use any brain power.

In affairs of the heart, you might think that dating websites would make things easier to land The One – giving each of us access to many more potential life-partners than we might otherwise meet in a lifetime – but does all this choice make it any easier to choose well?

Humans aren't anywhere near as keen on thinking as we ... tell ourselves we are.

If we have learned anything from the recent explosion of behavioural economics (BE), it's that we humans aren't anywhere near as keen on thinking as we (and the classical economists) tell ourselves we are. Indeed, to paraphrase Daniel Kahnemann, the Daddy of BE, *humans are to thinking as cats are to swimming* (we can do it if we really have to, but will try to avoid having to do so ...). While it has become a central tenet of modern life that more choice = better choice, the science will tend to disagree: more choice makes it harder to choose well.

Four different choice styles

Now take your piece of paper and mark up each of the quadrants in this way:

The central utility of this very simple map is that it allows us to plot different kinds of behaviour together and to see the connections and similarities between them (whether those behaviours are consumer buying patterns to the way we get our opinions about the world). But most of all, it allows us to see one thing as an example of a type or category of things. As a *kinda* thing...

Let's take a quick tour...

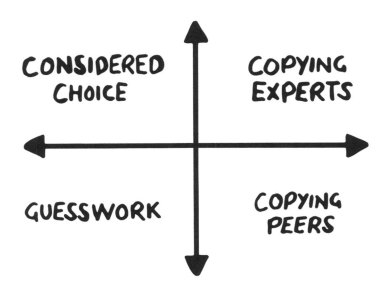

CONSIDERED CHOICE

In the North-West lies the kind of choice that might be typified as 'considered' or 'rational' choice (as the classical economists call it).

In other words, the choice has two key characteristics: first, individuals are choosing independently of each other and second, the qualities of the things being chosen from (their 'utility' as the jargon has it) are what matters most here.

In 'considered' choices, the thing itself is really important. Many manufacturing or tech businesses enjoy this model as a default setting – they would like the 'superiority of their thing' to be the determining factor. Vinyl junkies like to believe that this is what they're doing as they sift through specialist music stores for that version of a particular tune.

In the South-West is the kind of choice that might be characterized as 'guesswork'.

Here typically choices are between many indistinguishable items, the quality of which is largely acceptable. The television market is a good example here – all those large, thin black screens which have all the same functions and buttonry. Here *the thing* matters less – acceptable quality is effectively available from all the choices in the market – so the relative *salience* of the options one to another is vital in shaping the choice.

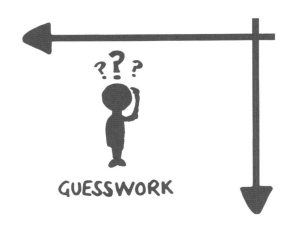

GUESSWORK

Behaviours shaped by habit and habituation are also located in this part of the map – the thing is less important than the ease of choosing. That is why for example so many consumer products that you might buy in a supermarket or grocery store live in this part of the map: they are things we buy over and over, through habit and similar low-level cognitive activity.

COPYING EXPERTS

By contrast, the North-East represents the kind of choice that is typified by *expert recommendation* or following the example of authoritative individuals.

Here the quality of the things being chosen may or may not be important but either way it's the behaviour, enthusiasm and recommendation of experts and others with relevant social status that matters in shaping individual choices. Typical of this kind of choice are high-end technology markets such as semi-pro cameras or professional recording equipment – where you really do need an expert to guide your choices. Another example all budding rock-musicians will recognize is that of the Marshall amplifier – while other brands of guitar amp are available (we are a mixed family in my band, The Big Shorts), no guitarist will challenge your choice of a Marshall. It's what guitar heroes/experts like Jimmy Page and Dave Gilmour choose, so it can't be bad, can it?

Finally, in the South-East, we see the kind of choice an individual might make by looking at those around them for guidance but in a much less directed or focused way. What matters here is the impression of what other people seem to be doing or doing more of.

Because the copying is unfocused on a particular person, this can make popularity unstable and unpredictable over time.

Apple are particularly good at popularity strategies – consider the white earbuds that come with Apple's music devices. Until recently these delivered pretty poor music quality for users but they served as a rather fantastic signal as to the popularity of Apple's devices in a market where the device itself (mp3 player) is often hidden.

COPYING PEERS

HOW CAN YOU LOCATE THE BEHAVIOUR ON THIS MAP?

For those of a more quantitative frame of mind, the data patterns that lie beneath the map are really useful in fixing the position of a particular behaviour or choice – the data can do the heavy lifting for you, rather than you merely having to rely on your own (and your colleagues') assumptions and prejudices.

Plotting W-E

You may remember the simple diffusion curves we drew in the discussion about how copying spreads things (see the 'iSpread' section on page 17). You can use these to plot how a specific brand or product spreads through a population over time. How many 'mavericks' or lone individuals are involved in the adoption of a particular behaviour (relative to all adopters) will help you place it on the West or the East of the map.

In practice, we tend to use a slightly different patterning in market- or population-level behaviour data – like sales figures or clicks (not least because it's very time consuming to examine each and every single product or choice). We simply plot out the popularity of each of the choices at any particular time 't' – what share each choice has of the total market.

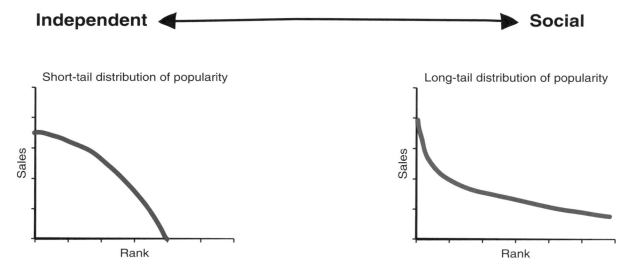

74

If (as you see on the right-hand curve) you see a long-tail of popularity emerge (where few items account for most of and most account for b- all of the market) then this is a strong signal that the behaviour is shaped by social influence and copying; otherwise, you're probably dealing with more independent choice (as indicated by the short-tail distribution of popularity).

Mapping N-S

This dimension of the map bakes in an important insight that is only now becoming popular with behavioural and cognitive scientists: that is, that most choices we make are not binary or A, B or C. Most decision-landscapes have many options – often a bewildering amount of options.

Think of it this way: your average supermarket is awash with options – 40,000, 50,000 or more individual products. Compare this to the mom-and-pop corner store our parents grew up with. It's just worth plotting the behaviour in terms of the number of choices available – knowing that the average European laptop market has some 3500 SKUs to choose from immediately suggests that this plots in the Southern part of the map.

But sometimes counting options is insufficient. Take alchoholic drinks for example: some are chosen consistently – it's very slow for new things to get adopted. Whisky has historically worked this way.

By contrast Vodka is as noisy as a teenager's party – new favourites coming in and vanishing again immediately without a trace. So in this kind of case, we also look at the speed of turnover of popularity as an indicator of where a behaviour is on the N-S dimension. The noisy up-and-down of popularity turnover plots that might otherwise confuse and distract tells us something much simpler and more important than who's in or out this week: it marks out this market as a Southern one. Knowing this is the background – default – choice style in a market, makes individual variances stand out. In the case of vodka, it helps separate the stayers from the One Night Stands. Which in turn might give you ideas about how to make a stayer.

Of course, there's much more to it than this. More nuance and more technique. For more detail on these patterns and how to tell them apart, please try *I'll Have What She's Having.*[52]

Here's a simple checklist to help you start doing this:

- Are people choosing from a small number of items or listening to the advice and example of a small number of experts? (NORTH)
- Are there many options to choose between? Is it hard to discern quality or expertise? Are there lots of options which are pretty good? (SOUTH)
- Are people choosing based on the quality of the thing (or whatever's salient)? (WEST)
- Or, are they choosing based on the opinions and choices of others? (EAST)
- Is the thing the thing, really? (NW)
- Is habit or salience or price really the thing? (SW)
- Is popularity and fashionability everything? (SE)
- Or, are experts, authorities and traditions essential to making your choice? (NE)

QUIZ TIME

Let's see how well I've explained this.

Let's return to the simple map you drew before (see opposite).

Now what I want you to do is identify where you think each of the following behaviours sits. (BTW it really helps if you actually draw the map and write the number of each behaviour where you think it belongs.)

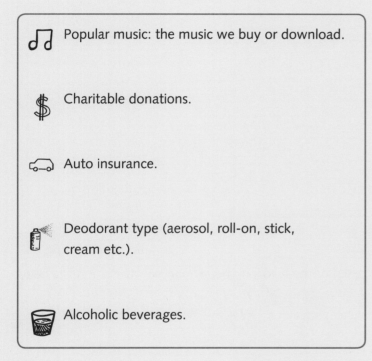

♫ Popular music: the music we buy or download.

$ Charitable donations.

🚗 Auto insurance.

🧴 Deodorant type (aerosol, roll-on, stick, cream etc.).

🥃 Alcoholic beverages.

No peeking now.

OK, so how did you do?

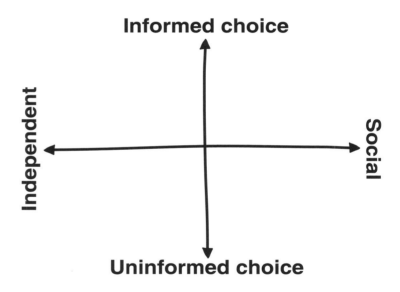

1. Popular music

As a lifelong music geek, I'd like to believe that the music itself matters – that better music will eventually work its way through to popularity. This would make the popular music a North-West phenomenon, rooted in considered choice.

Sadly, the experimental evidence from researchers like Duncan Watts, Matt Salganik and Peter Dodds[53] and the patterns that the sales charts exhibit point very strongly to this being a South-East phenomenon – popularity is more important to an artist's success than their talent or the quality of the music.

Popular music is a huge market with overwhelming choice (6 million+ songs on Spotify and 26 million+ on iTunes) so understandably, we think, people rely on what others have chosen as their guide. Not a particular person

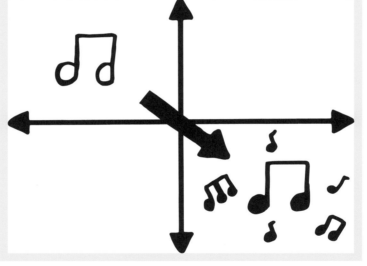

(as the self-styled music experts would have you believe) but what generally seems to be popular.

Susan Boyle has got a good voice and a memorable and tragic story but the truth is she got lucky in ALMOST winning *Britain's Got Talent* Series 3 (she came second) and going on to become one of the world's biggest recording artists. She became popular because individual buyers saw other buyers being excited about her – which is the premise of those talent shows like *Britain's Got Talent*. It also reveals the genius of Simon Cowell, using broadcasters' money to popularize the individuals he's signed up to his company until they are ready to launch a recording, thanks to this TV exposure paid for by somebody else.

2. Charitable donations

Of course, we'd all like to think that we select the charitable causes we donate to on the basis of personal connections (e.g. Cancer Research) or deep personal convictions (e.g. Oxfam) but the data suggest that charitable giving is largely a North-East phenomenon: it's based on doing what we think authorities and cultural norms say we should do. For example, in the US, the number one recipient of charitable funding is religion – church, synagogue, chapel, temple, mission, whatever. It is just such a large part of US culture – it seems that everybody does it. In some cultures – e.g. Jewish, Italian Catholic and Asian and Wall Street – fundraising is a strongly social and visible phenomenon (think how charity fundraising is embedded in social interactions). It's a condition of membership to attend dinners, drives, bakes and drinks.

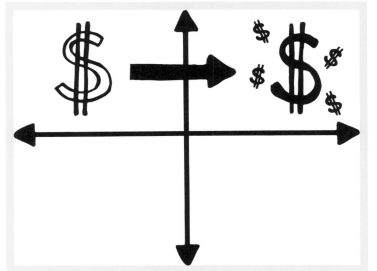

Similarly, the US number two is education. If, like Alex Bentley, you have been through the US education system, you will know that first you are a fundraiser then an alumnus or alumna. Alex holds degrees from three different US colleges and is thus a target for three different groups of fundraisers.

Of course, in the UK the preferences are different (we are a nation of animal lovers) but the patterns are the same: charity is a North-East phenomenon ('Copying experts').

And at the bottom end of the rankings, perceived popularity can be important (South-Eastern) but the majority of the money is distributed via copying experts (North-East).

3. Auto insurance

If you have bought some car insurance recently, we're almost certain that you didn't make a 'sound decision' – a 'good choice' as far as an economist would put it.

price ('that seems reasonable' and familiarity ('Oh, I've heard of THEM') and a host of other post-rationalizations ('they've been very good, haven't they?').

We're fairly sure you didn't consult all of the options in the market and compare them each one with another – most of us just renew our old policy or take up what seems like a good offer.

Nor will you have considered all of the dimensions of all the options available to you. Even armed with the shortlist generated by the computing power of a comparison website, most of us still choose on the basis of headline

Insurance – apparently the most rational of decisions given that it's all about the numericals – is definitely South-West ('Guesswork'). We just don't 'do the math', do we? Too many dimensions, too many choices – just too darn hard.

4. Deodorants

You may be wondering at this point where the role of the superior product is on our map. So far, none of the quadrants have featured the product; none has the product and its features as central to how people make their choices.

Buying deodorants is a reassuring exception: at least as far as deodorant *format* is concerned (stick, aerosol, roll-on etc. – deodorant brand choice can be different). Buyers have genuine product preferences – analysis of buying patterns over time tends to suggest that these are fairly stable preferences, however an individual came to use them.

And yet, every year some bright spark in the personal products team at Unilever, P&G or Colgate wakes up with idea that they can switch buyers up from lower margin formats like roll-ons to the higher margin aerosols. Unfortunately many of those who prefer roll-ons or some other form will switch out of their preferred brand to stay with the format they like rather than trade up.

There are course strategies to deal with this – merchandising and pricing have important roles to play in unpicking the central choice style but it is nevertheless remarkably stable.

Despite this being many people's default assumption about how most choices are made (whether it is by considering the comparative utilities of different items, as the economists put it or by 'feeling' an emotional connection or some such, as the psychologists put it) or indeed how they *should* be made (making a good decision demands lots of high level cognitive activity, doesn't it?), the truth is that it's much less common than we imagine – much, *much less* common.

5. Alcoholic beverages

Booze is a fundamentally Eastern phenomenon on our map, being shaped by social forces. 'I'll have what she's having' is a widely used shorthand all drinkers use.

Some North European cultures have long been beer-drinking cultures; others – like France – have long been wine-drinking cultures; others still (like the US) are strong spirits markets. The patterns of long-term change in alcohol consumption are also characteristically social, suggesting that the behaviour is embedded in culture and other traditional practices. For example, the long, slow decline in on-premises drinking in the UK are also indicative of the NE of our map.

What we drink is also shaped by culture: for example, rum was the original drink of the US Founding Fathers but now it is a minority choice beyond from the 'Atlantic Rim' – New England's coast line – and Hispanic Miami. Tequila by contrast is relatively popular in the South West of the States (where Hispanic culture holds strong) and much less so elsewhere.

Malt and whiskey drinking is clearly located in the NE – it often entails a degree of connoisseurship and knowledge. This is in stark contrast to vodka – widely accepted as the alcohol for people who don't like the taste of alcohol. Choice in vodka is more like pop music – SE popularity is all that counts. Apart from the few brands that break through and become social badges for specific groups (NE).

And, problem drinking and addiction is also highly social, whatever its genetic an biological roots: the biggest single predictor of whether or not an individual stays clean and sober after rehab is whether or not they return to their 'drinking' social network. No wonder, AA and the 12 step programmes place such emphasis on building up alternative social networks through mentoring and meetings.

VOTE FOR ME!

OK, let's walk through one final example that we discussed in the Introduction:

Where does *voting* sit on the map?

Draw yourself another map (see the earlier informed/uninformed axis map)

Is voting an *independent choice*, with each candidate's policies, track record and personality being weighed by individual voters – each voter considering the options and the issues carefully before coming to their own independent conclusion?

Or does *voting tend to be more social*? With people voting according to their tribal norms ('people like me') or according to their 'class'?

Are voters led by what's happening in the polls – what market research and the media tell them other people are doing or will do? Do they pay any attention to community activists or window and bumper stickers? Do they make their own minds up? Or are their voting patterns shaped by those around them?

Well, much as we'd like it to be the former, the truth is it's more likely to be the latter – even the long slow decline in the general public's engagement with party politics in the UK and elsewhere is likely to be a social rather than an individual phenomenon (like the decline in on-trade beer drinking observed just now).

We know we are easily led by the choices of others, which is why we go to such lengths to discourage it – from the privacy of the polling booth, the banning of opinion polls in the latter stages of elections (e.g. in Germany and India) to the suppression of exit polls until the polls are closed and all the votes are in and the discouraging of 'block voting' by religious groups and community leaders. And this is why we still like a good political rally and VOTE FOR ME lapel button (or Facebook Like).

Voting is social (both South-East and North-East) but we try ever so hard to make it independent and based on a considered judgement (North-West).

A DIFFERENT KIND OF MAP OF HUMAN BEHAVIOUR

One of the big differences behind this behaviour map and others is that with this one we make no specific assumption about how people actually choose. We are agnostic (which is not the case with maps built on specific disciplines).

For example, classical economists will draw the map like this with the North-West predominating:

They'll accept that sometimes people don't make 'good' decisions but still would prefer to believe that people calculate relative utilities of each option in front of them in order to optimize their choice (or that they should strive to do so). Your mum also would like to believe that you think about your choices as this suggests (although she knows – and you know she knows – that you do this rather less often than you tell her you do).

Behavioural economists ('Nudgers') who have primary interest in individual cognitive biases will tend to focus on the Western side of the map.

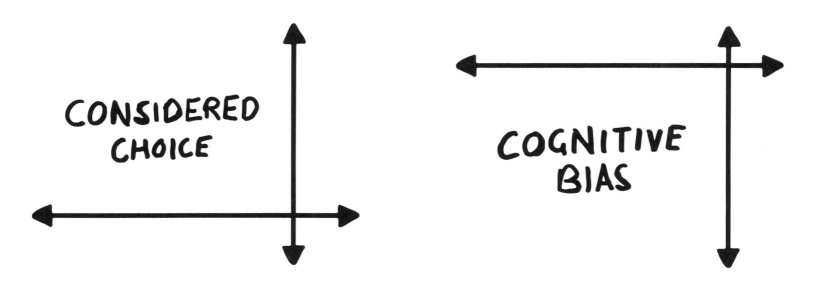

With some rare exceptions – for example, in discussing 'social proof' – BE fans tend not to look East. Even the otherwise excellent Mindspace Report, produced in 2010 for the UK Cabinet Office to improve policy making by harnessing insights from *Nudge* and similar books, was dominated by insights on the West of the map (only one in nine major insights was social in any sense).

By contrast, *word-of-mouth marketers* will tend to assume that the North-East will predominate in how people choose.

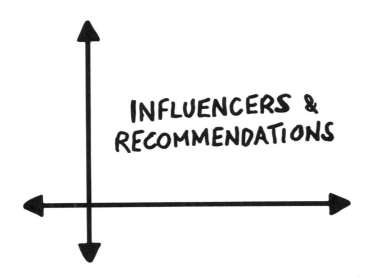

INFLUENCERS & RECOMMENDATIONS

As far as many WoM-ers are concerned, in most populations there will be key individuals – social hubs – to whom the rest of a population defer. This is sometimes the case but not as often as they/you might think.

We accept that sometimes at least each of these will be a good description of how a particular phenomenon is shaped, but not as often as their advocates would suggest.

Of course, I too have my own biases and assumptions. For example, my experience tells me that the Southern part of our map is more important than any of these schools would suggest. Choices in the modern world are not simple and binary: it's rarely just A or B or C. Nor is expertise always obvious or easy to isolate from all the noise out there (reading the reviews on Amazon, TripAdvisor or similar is exhausting nowadays – even the volume of recommendations is overwhelming).

Similarly, I am far more open to the possibility that any given decision or choice is in reality shaped primarily by *social forces* – by what goes on between individuals rather than by what occurs in the grey matter between an individual's ears. I've long argued that the importance of *social* has been suppressed in both theory and practice: we are a fundamentally social species and it should come as now surprise that many of our choices – big small or somewhere in between – should be *social choices*.

But I don't assume that this is the case of any given behaviour – a priori. Nor should you.

FROM A DESCRIPTIVE MAP TO A STRATEGY MAP …

Many of the people who've worked with the map tell us that they have found it a useful frame for starting to think about human behaviour.

It breaks the ground in thinking about any phenomenon, helping to chunk it out into simpler pieces.

And in doing so it facilitates and encourages more conversations about *what kind of thing?*, just as we intended.

That said, a number of people want to nuance the map, to make it more specific. This is as true of practitioners as social scientists: some want to add an extra dimension (3D must be better than 2D, no?) or adjust one of the scales to make it even more precise or to reflect their other concerns (this is popular amongst those on the theory end). Others again want to make it even more quantitative: one client was keen to develop a more granulated measurement of each dimension to satisfy their

Image reworked from http://commons.wikimedia.org/wiki/File:Karl_Marx.png

hunger for detail and to reduce the need for interpretation. Could we, they asked, create a way of producing precise co-ordinates for each item?

All of which is fine and dandy – and a good indication that the basic map is useful to the people it was created for – but…BUT…

The descriptive power of the map is only part of the story. Important but small.

Too much of time and effort in the insights world is spent on description – digging deeper and deeper and becoming more and more specific in description of The Singular Thing. Knowing ever more about It doesn't help you strategize or solve the problem – all too often, it's just an excuse for not getting to grips with what to do. Too much Think-Do and not enough Do.

As the grumpy German émigré, Karl Marx put it, while many smart folk have sought to describe the world with increasing precision, the point really is to change it.

WHERE NEXT?

The next chapter contains not just one answer but an veritable archive of answers to what to do next – what to copy.

It's arranged as a 'pattern-book' (or 'pattern-books' – there's one for each part of the map). Something to steal from and make your own.

At its heart are some of the very many successful strategies that my collaborators and I have observed over the years across many different fields and disciplines, sorted by 'what kind of thing?' groups described here. So it's much more than a listicle (a long list of things that work).

And to make it easy for you we've created a set of cards to help you play with these once you get used to doing so (CopyCopyCopy.co)

Anything that can get strategy closer to *doing*…

Drawing *is* thinking.

Drawing helps you work out the relationships between things.

Drawing our simple map and locating the behaviour you're targeting within it gives you a head start.

It helps you work out what kinda (kind of) thing you're dealing with.

And thereby helps you work out where to look for solutions to copy and steal

CONCLUSION

"So many books, so little time."

—Frank Zappa

What this chapter will cover:

When you know what kinda thing you're dealing, you're in a great place to work WHAT kind of strategies might serve you best.

This chapter contains our archive of 52 different kinds of strategy, sorted into the four quadrants of our map.

Each strategy is illustrated by 2-3 examples from a range of different contexts – marketing and behaviour change.

The point here is to make it easier for you to pick one or two (or three) to copy.

This kind of collection of ideas is most reminiscent of what the construction industry has long known as a "pattern book".

So that's where we start

4 WHERE TO COPY FROM: THE PATTERN BOOKS

52 different strategies to copy, borrow or steal

'INDOCILIS PRIVATA LOQUI'[54]

Let me tell you about a secret society which has long operated in the shadows of our world – just out of the corner of your eye, invisible to all but those who know where to look. All these years, this dark brotherhood has fiercely guarded the arcane wisdom and the secret books of know-how and knowledge collected by its members and passed down over many generations; ex-communicating (and even perhaps, you might suspect, executing) those who dare to share the forbidden truths. You might think we'd landed in a cloak-and-dagger Sherlock Holmes story, a Dan Brown novel or one of the darker parts of the conspiracy-washed internet.

As it happens, the society I have in mind is the Magic Circle – the official professional association of stage magicians and illusionists (they also welcome amateur members). Despite being a relatively young body (as far as these things go – it was founded as late as in 1908 in a small Italian restaurant in London's Soho), they seem to hold tight to the basic premises of the masonic world – arcana and oaths and a procession through levels of the organization up and in towards the 'elect' (the Inner Magic Circle). Each step you take is conditional that the secrets be kept. You must must MUST not tell – hence the motto 'Indocilis private loquis' (roughly translated as 'incapable of talking of private matters'). Schtumm! Or else.

Actually this secrecy piece is slightly overplayed: in the first 100 years of the society's existence only one member has been publicly ejected for revealing the precious secrets. American magician John Lenehan agreed to lift the lid on the card trick beloved of street hustlers and hucksters everywhere ('three card monte' AKA 'find the lady'). And on a BBC TV show, *How Do They Do That?* Out he went.

> ❝ **The best way to keep something secret is to hide it in plain sight.** ❞

But as any good illusionist knows, the best way to keep something secret is to hide it in plain sight. This is what the professional that you might more naturally imagine would play by 'masonic' rules: architects and builders (the original 'masons').

Architecture still likes to present itself in the familiar language of creativity originality – original (singular) building(s) based on original designs by (singular) creative geniuses such as Ayn Rand's fictional Howard Roark – the truth is that architecture and the whole construction industry has long used the work of others, collated and distributed as 'pattern books'. But while medieval masons and other historical forefathers of today's architects might have fought to keep these secret books and their know-how hidden from the rest of us, for six centuries and more, architecture's pattern books have been placed firmly in the public domain.

You may, like me, have admired the famous architectural drawings of masters such as the 16th Century Venetian, Andrea Palladio, whose 4 books of detailed illustrations (the 'Quattro libri') brought not just the style of the classics to Western Europe but also – perhaps more importantly – the ability to reproduce that style. His beautiful drawings

and designs – based on his own study and re-incorporation of the surviving Greek and Roman examples into his own projects – now adorn the walls of many a country house hotel and Stately Home. However, for his contemporaries and those who followed immediately, they represented a do-it-yourself kit in classical style: from the proportions, the way a façade or a dome or a window should look to the detail of plaster or other decoration – all of this in easy-to-use, cut-and-paste imagery.

" Pattern books have long been central to architecture and building. "

The 'Quattro Libri' were collected far and wide: for example, both England's Sir Christopher Wren (most famous perhaps for rebuilding London after the Great Fire of 1666) and Thomas Jefferson, 4th President of the USA and keen amateur architect, both had collections of Palladio's drawings and used them extensively as models in their own constructions. Neither found it at all embarrassing to use someone else's drawings as a start-point (rather than merely vague 'inspiration'). Jefferson not only built a fabulous mansion, Monticello, in the 'Palladian'

style but also oversaw the competition for building the new nation's signature buildings – the White House and the Capitol – under the heavy influence of the Italian. (Although the current version of the Capitol building is the product of a later rebuild, to an English eye, its dome roof still bears a striking resemblance to that of Wren's St Paul's Cathedral; both to a number of Palladio's Italian Churches).

The longstanding use of pattern books of one sort or another also explains why many historical towns and cities seem to have a particular 'look' or style. Georgian London, Dublin and Bath enjoy the style they do because Georgian pattern books were particularly well put-together and practical. Some even provided tables to enable the generic floor plan and design to be adjusted according to the plot size, the building height and the target demographic. And yet at the same time, they provided the means for variation in smaller details of decoration so that the whole design remained characteristically harmonious.

> ❝ **Georgian London and Dublin look the way they do because of pattern books.** ❞

In the 18th and 19th Centuries, pattern-booking was hugely popular in the US, too, which explains why American historic city centres often have an internally consistent style 'Famous pattern books were created by Andrew Jackson Downing, for example, known for his romantic cottage designs; Minard Lafever, who detailed Greek-inspired proportions; and William T. Comstock, who promulgated Victorian patterns.'[55] Organizations like Sears, Roebuck & Company made a fortune sharing pattern books to the aspiring American middle classes in the 20th Century, too.

> ❝ **In the US, pattern booking shaped how many historic city centres still look.** ❞

METROLAND

The style of buildings in our much derided suburbs tell the same story. Take for example the archetypal 'mock Tudor' style of Early and Mid 20th Century British suburbia, with its white washed walls, extruding bay windows, leaded glass lights and – most characteristic of all – the exposed black-stained beams. We children of the suburbs have come to take it for granted that our shops and homes should be dressed so theatrically but I've long thought all of this heavily accented built history must be quite striking to the foreign visitor – evoking the dreams of the Ye Olde World England ('Shakespearland -just like I pictured it').

Certainly, that was the intention of property developers like the Metropolitan Railway Board, who invented the marketing concept of 'Metroland' to lure out Londoners from the dark, damp tenements to which they had returned after the first world war. The Board sold the land off in relatively small parcels to small-time developers who copied and reinterpreted what had started as a high-end architectural style of sylvan idyll into a simple-to-repeat recipe that still made the same promise (albeit on a smaller plot and budget to match).

As time went on, and more areas were developed, those doing the building adapted and evolved the pattern book again and again so that the vast estates built in the 1930s and 1940s only bear rudimentary references back to the original pattern books. But each still delivers a version – albeit a somewhat diluted version – of that original promised escape to the country and to a kinder, safer place ('Merrie England' as Kingsley Amis derided it in Lucky Jim).

PATTERN BOOKS AND ORIGINAL BUILDINGS

Later, as we walked and talked, Alistair underlined the importance of pattern books even for the most celebrated and 'original' modern architects. Berthold Lubetkin's Grade 1 Listed Highpoint building in Highgate, North London is a modernist dream, built in the International style and thus unlike many of the buildings it is surrounded by. Alistair's students at RIBA imagine that this jewel of London's 20th-Century architecture was conceived as an act of independent creative will. The truth is that Lubetkin worked really closely with the pattern book then in force with Highgate's planning department. He just happened to reinterpret and play with almost all of the details.

" You don't want to have to rethink every aspect…each time you break ground. "

Consider this from a purely practical perspective. Why start with having to rethink every aspect of a building from scratch – its design, its function. Its decoration and its relationship with other parts – each time you break ground. Why not make it easy on yourself – as builders and architects have always done – and start with the givens. Copy first, vary second.

TERN BOOKS EVERYWHERE

The more you think about pattern books, the more you see pattern books. The more you see pattern books, the more you see pattern-booking behaviour.

What else is our collective obsession with make-over shows, with cooking and recipe books and shows (often conceived together) but pattern-booking? Interior design is the same – with TV shows, magazines, blogs and (yes, indeed) endless room-sets in stores or in the ubiquitous IKEA catalogue.

Since the first fashion plate books spread around Europe and the New World in the 19th Century, pattern-booking has been one of the ways in which we make our choices in this aspect of our life.

Today's fashion and celebrity magazines continue to encourage the same behaviour with their photography and features. Indeed, most don't even shy away from showing us how to put together a particular look, using explicit comparisons of fashion runway and high street versions of the same thing.

> **The more you think about pattern books, the more you see pattern books.**

When you read that an event or exhibition claims to 'celebrate excellence', it's odds to evens that the audience for that event is using the examples presented as a pattern book, albeit in walk-through form.

This struck me forcefully when, in the summer of 2013, the esteemed Royal Horticultural Society's Chelsea Flower Show celebrated its centenary. To the organizers it was a showcase for all that's good in British garden design and plantsmanship; to the vast majority of visitors it offered the world's largest walk-through treasure trove of ideas, techniques and plants to make/remake our gardens ('a water feature, some of those ferny things and a slate-path, maybe?'). Any industry body collecting, judging and displaying the best work of its practitioners is doing the same thing.

Our weekend visits to the great gardens of the National Trust are not merely to explore and celebrate the unique designs of each gardener but also to provide ideas on what to steal next. Not only do you get to buy the souvenir tea towel but take home some planting or landscaping ideas, too. Whatever the intentions of those designing and creating the garden, it's what we visitors do with it that matters – how we use it.

Whatever the creator's intentions, it's what we do with the things we use as pattern books that matters.

In some cases, the 'pattern book' purpose of an individual collecting disparate musical work is easier to spot. In the 1980s, at the birth of hip-hop, a New York City cab driver, one DJ Breakbeat Lenny, created a series of illicit albums of drum samples. These became the pattern book for much of hip-hop and contemporary dance music (especially breaks like 'Amen Break', five seconds of rhythm clipped from the B-side of an obscure R&B single by the Winstons). Not only did hip-hop DJs use the samples on the 'Breakbeat' albums as their stock in trade, so too did other musicians (the Amen Break itself is the rhythmical basis of the British styles of Drum and Dubstep while at the same time providing colour to songs by artists as far away as Oasis' Gallagher brothers). Jamaican music of the 1970s and 1980s often featured a 'version' or 'dubplate' on the flipside – instrumental versions of the featured tune which encourage similar hybridizations.

Pattern booking almost guarantees 'good' (i.e. bad) copying.

What's particularly powerful about a pattern book is that it almost guarantees 'good' (i.e. bad) copying from the audience: my garden is 'inspired by' a number of places I have visited, including the cool indigo blues of the Yves St Laurent garden in Marrakech and the dark and fern-fringed corners of Heligan and Kew's own glasshouses. By combining bits of each and placing them in a new context, the new thing can't help but become something different from all and any of the things that inspired it.

The internet has provided great scope for those who want to seek 'inspiration' from others: in many ways, what the internet is all about is pattern-booking. From Piers Fawkes' New York City-based PSFK to William Rowe's supercool Protein network and the fabulous and wonderfully named Rubbishcorp.com curated by Nathan Cooper – the creative industries have an endless supply of interesting stuff to beg, borrow and steal right there on their smartphones (if it's still OK to have a smartphone, now that my Dad has one). Just lean back on the sofa and window shop for inspiration on your iPad or iPhone.

BETTER

Considered choices need **better** strategies – rooted in real or perceived superiority of your thing over other choices.

'I QUATTRI LIBRI'

This section comprises our archive – our 'quattri libri' – of successful strategies and examples for you to copy and use as the basis of your behaviour change programmes, all sorted by the four 'kinda' choice styles.

SALIENCE

Guesswork choices need **salience** strategies. Don't make the chooser think and don't worry about the thing being better, but rather make it easier to choose by making it stand out from competing options.

EXPERTISE

Choices based on **Copying Experts or Authorities** demand strategies based on **expertise** or **authority**. Because he/she likes, endorses, enthuses over the choice, the quality of the choice must be clear.

POPULARITY

Finally, choices shaped by **Copying peers** demand strategies based on real or perceived **popularity**. Because everyone's doing it, why don't I do it, too?

Who lives here?

If nothing else, this simple frame can help set your thinking going faster than before. However, most of us respond well to specific examples rather than high-level abstract thoughts, so we reviewed the examples of successful strategies we had observed under each of these headings.

Our first sort created more than 120 different examples. But to make these books easier to use, we then grouped two to three examples together under the type of strategy they represent. This still creates more than 52 different kinds of strategy, spread across the four choice styles – a lot, but far more manageable. And entirely appropriate for the pack of cards we have produced to help you use the archive more easily!

CopyCopyCopy.co

97

THE STRATEGIES

HOW TO USE THE PATTERN BOOKS

We don't suggest you try reading all of these
in one go – even now there are far too many
to process at one sitting. However, we suggest
you flip through and return when you're faced
with a particular problem – as you will be in the
following chapter!

If nothing else please use the opening description
for each group of strategies as a reminder of the
'kind of thing' you're dealing with.

It is also worth saying that this archive is not
exhaustive – so please feel free to suggest new
kinds of strategies and examples as you discover
them.

BETTER

EXPERTISE

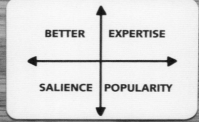

BETTER | EXPERTISE

SALIENCE | POPULARITY

SALIENCE

POPULARITY

CONSIDERED CHOICE: 'BETTER' STRATEGIES

BETTER

In the North-West part of the map, people are choosing independently of each other on the basis of the utility or quality (real or perceived) of what's in front of them. It's the rare case of the product's superiority or perceived superiority being at the centre of how individuals choose.

Strategies here have to be rooted in BETTER – in managing perceptions of better, creating new kinds of better or new ways of calibrating or demonstrating better.

A lot of these will be familiar because Considered Choice is still the default assumption of many marketers (particularly those in manufacturing businesses whose culture is rooted in the real or perceived quality of things the factory creates) and many policy makers (just tell them why they should do it!). For some, indeed, this will be what marketing is all about. If that is you, please hold on: other effective strategies are available – later on in this chapter.

DRAMATISE BETTER

GIVE THE PRODUCT AWAY TO PROVE BETTER

HIGHLIGHT A SURPRISING REASON FOR BETTER

INVENT A NEW DIMENSION FOR BETTER

LINK YOUR ORIGIN TO YOUR SUPERIORITY

BETTER

BETTER MOUSETRAP

Dyson & Walkman are clearly better products (but better doesn't...
New...

THE ORIGINAL...

Levi Strauss are the original jean, and Mini the original small ...the "...ators"

TORTURE TEST

Detergent and dishwasher tablet brands are very inventive at finding ways to demo better. Polycell (wallpaper paste) stuck a man to a biplane to test adhesion.

BUILD A BETTER MOUSETRAP

This is the go-to option for the engineering mindset and for all those who want to believe that people are 'utility optimizers' (i.e. they want to buy the best). This is particularly common amongst those who work in the factory or the design studio, in our experience. Dyson's household appliances are a great example of a business that uses this strategy as its core one: the way for a small business to beat bigger businesses is to make a better product, surely? Well, maybe but it's expensive and success is far from guaranteed, not least because 'better' is the not only way people buy.

When Coke sought to overcome the longstanding disadvantage that taste-tests showed the core product, 'Red' Coke, suffered compared to Pepsi, they launched a new product, 'New Coke'. This proved a disaster – not only losing lots of customers but also their goodwill ('we like the old Coke, why did you change it?'). In addition, the corporation took a long while to get its confidence back.

Not to be outdone, Pepsi had their own better mousetrap hiccup recently when they used one of the US's most famous and talented packaging designers to redesign Tropicana fruit juice packs with a similarly disastrous outcome: sales plummeted and phone lines flamed as customers failed to recognize their brand (the brilliant new packaging made it look more like store own label and disappear into the visual field of the chiller cabinet).

THE ORIGINAL (AND THEREFORE THE BEST)

Being the original in any market is a good short hand for quality – no 'mucking around', no manipulation by cynical marketing guys. Original things have stood the test of time – this makes them familiar and credible at the same time.

Levi-Strauss have exploited this in the apparel market over many years, being 'the original jean' although it must be said that they have sometimes been blindsided by the shifting culture and what it determines 'jeans' are (they failed to see the emergence of 'baggy' denim, entirely).

CREATE A NEW TEST OF BETTER

Detergent brands have always been very inventive at finding ways to demo their cleaning performance better. Whether it's holding a clean white shirt up to the light or leaving a sock in the pocket which also gets 'deep down clean', the history of detergent marketing has many great examples to steal.

But this is not just an advertising copy route. PJ Barnum – the great circus entrepreneur – was fond of finding new and memorable ways to demonstrate the brilliance of his shows as his big tent went from town to town.

What do you think he would do to demonstrate the superior sticking power of a new wallpaper glue? Stick a man to a plane and then fly it about?

That's exactly what Polycell did in the UK.

USE HIGH PRICE TO SIGNAL BETTER

Luxury brands are past-masters at using eye-watering price points to suggest quality. If it is THAT expensive it must be better. Nowadays, of course, copies of luxury goods are readily available – most magazines and newspapers will have a chic vs. cheap fashion strand, in which the luxury and the high street are put side-by-side. Even so, many people would choose the high-priced luxury if they could.

Of course as markets become more and more saturated, luxury retailers can take a further step up the price ladder by failing to indicate price at all on the basis that if you need to look at the price you can't afford to shop there!

GIVE THE PRODUCT AWAY SO THAT PEOPLE CAN SEE THE DIFFERENCE FOR THEMSELVES

Facebook and your local drug dealer have this strategy in common: they're more than happy to start by giving you away their product for free, knowing that you'll come to rely on it. Only then can they start really charging you for it.

Free product trial is great if you create this kind of appreciation of your product and how good it is, but for products that are an acquired taste (e.g. Campari), this can be counterproductive.

EMOTIONAL BENEFIT OF BETTER

It's increasingly clear even to those in the most engineering-minded businesses (like automotive) that their consumers' choices are not purely rational. BMW – that paragon of German engineering and design – has become increasingly focused on what its cars make you *feel* rather than what they do. 'Joy' is their watchword. This kind of strategy is strongly supported by fans of behavioural economics – to paraphrase one advocate, 'the more they feel, the more they buy'.

Another great example of this, but working in the opposite direction, is Converse's focus on 'dirty sneakers' as opposed to 'clean shoes'.

This is almost always a much better strategy for financial services than giving customers the information to make a sound, considered decision. As the behavioural economists like to point out, we are far more like Star Trek's Captain James T Kirk than his First Officer, the half-Vulcan, Mr Spock: more emotional than rational, more intuitive than considered.

FOCUS ON A SURPRISING REASON FOR BETTER

To the illogical human mind, surprise can be a much stronger lever than facts. The bright orange Scottish soft drink Irn Bru is supposedly 'made in Scotland from girders'. Avis built their business on the back not of being the biggest or the original but curiously by not being either of those things but wanting to be. 'We try harder' is all about the surprising virtues of being number 2.

INVENT A NEW DIMENSION OF BETTER

In the UK, Mars' Milky Way (a different product to the US candy bar of the same name) was originally pitched and made famous by being a 'lighter' snack that 'you can eat between meals' (rather than one which might satisfy a man's hunger which is how the same company's Snickers bar is now pitched).

In the USA, Audi have made inroads with their diesel engines (not as well established as they are in Europe) by suggesting that their fuel efficiency makes them a patriotic choice. In Spain, they've used their 'Quattro' 4WD system to create a different dimension of 'better' in high-end saloon cars.

The shift in the food movement from 'organic' to 'local' created a whole new dimension of better and one which chimed strongly with local identities and pride.

SCARCITY: RESTRICT SUPPLY TO EMPHASIZE BETTER

Scarcity is a great way to make something seem more attractive and valuable. The Blues Brothers famously played 'for one night only' and Bernd Pichetsrieder, the great BMW marketing guru insisted on 'always selling one less than you can'.

This kind of strategy is sometimes called the 'velvet rope' – 'you can't come in' often makes something that much more appealing. This was also the trick behind the story of how Frederick the Great turned Prussia into a potato eating nation – he insisted that no-one but the nobility could eat the potato. The 'aspirational' root vegetable? Believe it.

QUANTIFY BETTER

People love a simple relative scale, rather than absolute numbers. This kind of strategy uses our hazy connection with numbers to suggest better. Domestos kills 99% of all household germs; Broadband suppliers offer two, three or ten times faster service; and Compaq once claimed their laptops were cheaper over a lifetime ('costs you less than cheaper computers').

LINK YOUR ORIGIN TO SUPERIORITY

The French wine industry invented the notion of 'terroir' to justify the variance in quality that different landscapes and soils can have on the same product. It turns out to be largely nonsense – wine experts repeatedly fail to spot the right location – but it's still part and parcel of the conversation around fine wine.

German car manufacturers like Volkswagen have long exploited the stereotypical associations of quality that their origin brings, using German taglines like 'das Auto' in English-language marketing materials.

More humorously, the idea that happy cows make better butter has served New Zealand Dairy Farmers well for a number of years; more recently 'Happy Hens' became the shorthand to justify premium price eggs in the UK.

Schweppes justified their premium-priced answer to the new breed of 'artisan' tonic waters by launching a super-premium alternative themselves, with a new bottle based on one found on the Titanic. How's that for origin?

GUARANTEE SATISFACTION

In the UK, the John Lewis department stores have long offered a price promise to match competitive prices – 'never knowingly undersold'.

When I bought my first jalopy, manufacturing quality was not great so one-year warranties were sought after. Now three- or five-year warranties, even on second hand vehicles, are common. Kia now offer seven years – far longer than the average re-purchase cycle – as standard. This suggests a great deal of confidence in the product: it's a strong signal of quality.

The excellent Hardy of Alnwick (for what it's worth, my favourite fishing tackle manufacturer) offer lifetime repair and replacement on their exquisite and expensive hand-made fly fishing equipment. Each item is individually registered with them.

FORCE COMPARATIVE TRIAL TO DEMO BETTER

Pepsi's classic 'taste test' is a great example of using a comparative trial to gain customers, but you do need to be sure triallists will prefer yours to their existing choice.

Detergents have long used this as a mainstay of their advertising but there have been suggestions that – given the increasingly marginal differences in product performance in many categories – this is more a symbolic demonstration of better than a functional one.

Automotive dealerships are keen on getting prospects to test drive the new vehicle – not least because most new car buyers are selling an old car (with three to five-year-old technology and finish) and the comparison of new and old only has one likely winner.

DRAMATICALLY OVER-ENGINEER BETTER

This is one of the signature trends in modern marketing: 20 years ago, SUVs were a minority working vehicle, now few school runs are without vehicles capable of competing in and completing the Paris-Dakar Rally. The same is true of the wristwatch business – while the elegantly simple and the cheap and simple are still around, the explosion of diving or aviator watches worth thousands of dollars (often worth more than a car) is remarkable.

Indeed, the over-engineering of leisure clothing is legion – from sportswear to expeditionary equipment. These 'extreme' outdoor clothing brands are popular at a local North London bus stop: North Face, Annapurna and Patagonia. Being good enough to climb mountains in or wade mighty rivers in makes them ideal for any challenges you might encounter on the 29 bus (or even the 253).

DRAMATIZE BETTER

This is a frequently used ploy in advertising and communication: the Energizer Bunny and Sony's award-winning 'balls' commercial are both attempts to dramatize what better looks like for the audience: the first on an ongoing basis and the latter as a one-off.

Hardy of Alnwick have used a video of a huge shark being caught on one of the new-fangled trout rods (built for a much smaller fish) based on super-strength carbonfibre to do the same kind of thing, and show the surprising strength of the new rod.

Brand names often use this kind of strategy: think of 'extra', 'super' or similar epithets attached to a generic name.

GUESSWORK: 'SALIENCE' STRATEGIES

SALIENCE

In the South-West part of the map (Chapter 3), individuals are faced with a large number of indistinguishable options of acceptable quality. Repeated purchases can become a habit but the key is that there is little or no considered thought applied to the choice.

Successful strategies here are all rooted in SALIENCE – short-cutting considered decision making by various means (price, availability, changing the default etc.). A lot of Nudge strategies live here. Equally, the grocery marketer will find many of these strategies familiar – including the kind of promotional techniques that are the bread-and-butter of grocery marketing and communication.

MAKE IT EASIER TO CHOOSE YOU

MAKE IT HARDER TO LEAVE YOU

MAKE IT HARDER TO CHOOSE SOMEONE ELSE

REWARD THOSE WHO HAVE CHOSEN YOU BEFORE

MAKE IT EASIER TO CHOOSE YOU

SALIENCE

SALIENCE

SHOUT LOUDER

Use celebrities. Spend more on advertising. Make famous advertising.

HIGHLIGHT NEGATIVES

Financial penalties applying if you don't act now. The DFS furniture sale th__ __t end Monday'. Earlyb__ tomo__ Final __

SEEK FAME AT ALL COSTS

Ryanair will be controversial, Coke/Bud will be ubiquitous. Financial service brands focus on fame e.g. HSBC "global".

SEEK FAME AT ALL COSTS

Ryanair will be controversial and seek to get advertising banned wherever it flies. In Spain, the Desigual apparel brand has had great success by encouraging young women to rebel and reject the conservative expectations older Spanish culture has of them. For example, they've encouraged people to have morning sex and even gave away a small vibrator with their new fragrance.

French Connection tried the same kind of thing, with the (provocative) use of their FCUK logo. South West Airlines encourage their staff to do things that get talked about by customers. Richard Branson is an attention magnet for Virgin. Financial services brands often focus on awareness as the primary objective of their marketing (hence their widespread use of sports sponsorship).

SHOUT LOUDER

Spend more on your marketing. Use celebrities for no other reason than they get attention – both Gap and the UK's favourite retailer M&S have repeatedly used this strategy.

MAKE IT EASIER TO CHOOSE YOU

This seems obvious but availability is a very important cognitive factor in shaping consumer decisions: prominent (even garish) beer fonts simplify choice in a crowded bar. Heineken have recently taken to installing extra cold pumps that tower nearly a metre over the bar itself.

Preloaded software (from MS DOS to Internet Explorer) makes the choice of which to use a non-choice.

Behavioural economics has much to say in the area of 'resetting the default'. Lots of studies have shown that to encourage saving, it is far better not to make people opt in (they won't); instead, make saving the default and force them to opt out. Equally, while giving persuasive arguments to quit cigarette smoking can have some impact, this is nothing compared to the effect of banning smoking in the workplace.

REWARD THOSE WHO HAVE CHOSEN YOU BEFORE

This is the territory of frequent flyer miles and benefits, loyalty cards and loyalty discounts but also of thank you notes and RAOKs (random acts of kindness).

One great variation we found recently was on behalf of a group of independent coffee shops in Amsterdam who treated each other's customers as their own and rewarded them alike.

It is, however, worth bearing in mind that you are giving away profit with such activities and perhaps even teaching your customers to care primarily/only about these rewards. You can also create an extra layer of complication and another focus for customer frustration.

MAKE IT HARDER TO CHOOSE ANYONE ELSE

Ubiquity also means effective exclusivity. This is why beverage brands like Coke and Budweiser buy distribution or pouring rights in cinemas, sports arenas and so on.

Unilever built their old frozen food and ice cream businesses by installing fridges in retail outlets. Coke did the same with Coke branded refrigerators in gas-station forecourts.

MAKE IT HARDER TO LEAVE

The huge wealth of Apple's app ecosystem makes it really hard for customers to leave them for Android devices.

Auto renewals are the default on services like Amazon Prime or similar. These are now widespread in the insurance industry.

Some service providers like telephone companies or Cable TV suppliers have become notorious for making it hard to close accounts; or, they wait until you're absolutely determined to leave before setting their win-back team onto customers. Which is, of course, immensely annoying to customers but can – sometimes, at least – work to the company's advantage.

During the autumn of 2013, while a huge political storm blew up around energy prices in the UK, less than 5% of all households switched supplier.

Others – for example, UK energy companies – have a charging model which means that customers are always in arrears which puts a further break on their willingness to leave.

USE AGGRESSIVE PRICE POINTS TO DRIVE CHOICE

One of the ways to cut through crowded markets is aggressive pricing. News International has long used uneconomic pricing points over long periods to squeeze market share and margin out of competitors' hands.

Grocery stores regularly promote sharp pricing on KVIs (Known Value Items) to drive traffic from their competitors on the same basis.

PRIZES AND COMPETITIONS

This is another well tried strategy – not just from the Reader's Digest and other subscription-based businesses. Spain's most successful ever promotion is Nescafe's 'salary for life' ('Un sueldo … para toda la vida'). Other mainstream brands use this kind of strategy repeatedly without giving quite so much money away: Fritolay/Walkers has regular new flavours competitions. Candy brands have now started doing the same thing.

EYE-WATERING DISCOUNTS AND EVENTS

Related to this, the use of discounts and discount-based events is also powerful in driving short-term sales. This includes traditional promotions as well as Black Friday and Cyber Monday. It can also be more thematic, like American Express' Small Business Saturday.

PROMOTE AN UNUSUAL AND IRRELEVANT FEATURE

The mainstream beer market has been prone to this for some time. In the US, there was a phase when the nature Appalachian water used to brew with was a point of difference. In the UK, we had 'widgets' in cans to recreate the qualities of draught beer.

COLLABORATE WITH NON-COMPETITIVE BRANDS AND COMPANIES

The Bacardi and Coke probably helps Bacardi as much if not more than it does Coke. The UK Tourist Authority, Visit Britain, recently collaborated with Black's Outdoor Outfitters on a 'where to go/what to wear' programme for homestay holidays.

Airlines, car hire firms and hotel chains all go to market together and introduce each other's customers to their 'preferred partners' as part of their standard MO.

HIGHLIGHT COST OF DELAY

Don't make people think about the decision – focus on the financial penalties that delay will bring. E.g. That (endless) furniture sale that 'must end Monday'. Or on the money you save on that cruise but only if you act *now*.

COPYING EXPERTS: 'EXPERTISE' STRATEGIES

EXPERTISE

In this North-Eastern quadrant people are choosing based on the choices, enthusiasms and recommendations of a small number of individuals with recognized expert or authority status. Also included here are choices based on tradition and choices embedded in cultural practices (i.e. long dead experts and authorities).

It's worth remembering that the utility or benefits of the options being considered may or may not be important. For example, things that spread through Bass diffusions – a special kind of pattern of social adoption identified by Frank Bass and first published in 1963 – have inherent qualities that are learned about from experts and authorities (when you talk of 'early' or 'late' adopters this is the root). That said, the real power comes from the endorsement (tacit or explicit) of the 'influential' individual or group, rather than the qualities of the thing itself.

This is why strategies in this part of the map are all rooted in EXPERT and AUTHORITY – in harnessing the influence of a small number of respected individuals and in managing and supporting social identities.

IDENTIFY THE NEXT
GENERATION OF
EXPERT USERS

BE A BADGE
OF BELONGING

FIND SOCIAL
STRUCTURES OR
IDENTITIES TO
SUPPORT

MAKE ADVOCATES
OF EXPERT USERS
AND AUTHORITIES

LINK TO OTHER
CULTURAL
PRACTICES

EXPERTISE

EXPERTISE

SHARED CULTURE

Boots "Here come the girls" lauds
female office workers

EXPERT MAKERS

Sundance Festival was fronted by
Robert Redford for many years.
Chefs
ingre
cube

NEW KIND OF EXPERT

Camel was once marketed as the
doctor's choice of cigarette.
Carhartt/Timberland both
celebrate real workers in their
marketing.

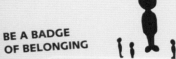

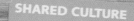

FIND EXPERT MAKERS TO ENDORSE YOUR CHOICE

The 'choice of the expert maker' has a lot of mileage in many contexts. Sundance Film Festival is brilliant and has become very influential in the movie business. However, it wouldn't have had half the traction if it had been fronted by someone other than Robert Redford. Justin Beiber might draw a crowd but what does he know about film-making?

Equally, Dr Dre may not have made a record for years, but his endorsement of Beats International's headphones provides a level of credibility they'd otherwise struggle to find, however good the headsets are.

littleBits is an open source library of electronic modules that snap together to make prototypes or educational models. Who better to endorse the 'space kit' than the people who brought you the Apollo missions, NASA?

DEFINE A NEW OR SURPRISING KIND OF EXPERT USER OR AUTHORITY

Camel cigarettes were once marketed as the doctor's choice of smoke (rather than that of the actors that other brands were prone to use).

The Hoffman Process – an intensive personal development programme – has used the endorsement of Elle Decoration's Editor-in-Chief Michelle Ogundehin (clearly an expert in a different kind of change) and the previously troubled musician and actor Goldie (ditto) alongside more traditional expert advocates such as psychotherapist Oliver James.

A number of apparel brands have moved beyond metaphor and use real workers in their 'workwear' product marketing. Carhartt even went as far as trying to reskill Detroit's young unemployed.

MAKING ADVOCATES OF EXPERT USERS AND OTHER AUTHORITIES

Nikon have long supported the pro-photographer community and provided its members with platforms to display their work and celebrate their skills. Auto firms are strongly dependent on a handful of journalists (Jeremy Clarkson in the UK) and invest heavily in these relationships.

The endorsement of beauty editors or make-up artists can give both profile and credence to a new skin or make-up product.

Brands that use expert founder stories also work this way – the pasta brand Rana makes much of the maestro pasta-maker, Giovanni Rana, whose name it bears.

IDENTIFY THE NEXT GENERATION OF EXPERT USERS

In many markets, the accepted experts are already taken. Sony's work in the camera market has focused more on the upcoming than established photographic experts. Their World Photography Awards celebrate the work and talent of the next generation and give them a platform.

MAKE YOURSELF PART OF A SHARED CULTURE OR IDENTITY

Marketers have long used user-image ('who is this for?' 'what kind of person buys or does this?') to link themselves to a cultural identity that audiences can easily understand and work with. Increasingly the social identity that you offer a prospect can help them.

However, given how marketing-savvy many people are nowadays, and how easily this social identity piece slips into stereotyping, you have to genuinely be committed to your chosen community and act accordingly. One good example is Lay potato chips who have recently focused on supporting local potato farmers and local school sports – a strategy which has huge attractions for the sales organization – even if the product promise it is built on (made from potatoes grown no more than 50 miles from the point of purchase) is particularly hard for the supply-chain to work with.

La Casera is one of those great local soft-drink brands which defies the hegemony of the Cokes and the Pepsis in their endless quest for new customers. It is the traditional Spanish brand, drunk on its own or mixed with wine ('tinto de Verano') or with beer ('Clara' or 'Rubia'). As Spanish as, well, La Casera.

FIND SOCIAL STRUCTURES OR IDENTITIES TO SUPPORT

Many US visitors to the UK find it hard to believe that Heinz (a Pittsburgh, Pennsylvania-based family business) has managed to position itself here as being as British as roast beef and bowler hats. So British does it seem in fact that the company managed to create a rumpus during the build-up to the 1998 Soccer World Cup by suggesting that the England team were being denied their natural food at training camp – Heinz Beans(z).

Equally, Apple have supported their developer community over many years – so much so that the late Steve Jobs made most of his major product announcements at developer (rather than consumer) events.

Converse have long supported live music in the UK, particularly at the grungier end of things. So when they heard that one of London's most iconic rock venues, the 100 Club, was due to close thanks to a rent rise, they intervened to support their community of guitar fans.

ROOT YOURSELF IN A SHARED CULTURAL TRUTH

Culture is the stuff that we all swim in – it's the shared assumptions and practices we all use to navigate our social world with. One classic marketing positioning strategy is to focus on (or 'own') a key cultural construct and celebrate and support it. Axe/Lynx's celebration of the adolescent male desire to be irresistibly attractive to women is one such strategy. Bacardi's recent focus on 'togetherness' or being 'untameable' also illustrates this.

GIVE PEOPLE SOMETHING TO DO WHICH BRINGS THEM TOGETHER

Human beings are very social creatures, so giving people things which bring them together around passions is often more useful than the products themselves.

Coke gave the game-crazy Hong Kong population a cell phone game called Choc Choc ('quick quick') to play against each other.

Crufts Dog Show – the Horse of the Year Show for the Kennel Club – was long ago turned into a national TV event, primarily through the sponsorship of Mars' Pedigree brand, which benefited from a long and consistent collaboration. Innocent Drinks invited all their customers to join them at Fruitstock (like a country fair in a London park). Even services which allow people to buy and sell from each other are often pursuing this strategy unwittingly, like AirBnB.

GIVE THEM SOMETHING TO BELIEVE IN

Dove's landmark Campaign for Real Beauty is far more than an advertising theme. It's an acknowledgement at a profound level that the beauty industry often makes women feel bad about their bodies and themselves. For the marketer this involves education programmes, campaigning and lobbying as well as presenting products in more women-friendly ways.

IBM has managed to reposition itself as more than another tech giant by envisioning the future – first with e-business and now with Solutions for a Smarter Planet.

People really do like to believe in things – this kind of 'purpose-idea' is a flag for people to gather round and be together.[56]

TRANSLATE YOUR AGENDA INTO THEIR AGENDA

The green movement – like many who want to change the world in a particular way – has long struggled in trying to win a philosophical – or rather a 'theological' – argument with people who don't agree with them.

Laying out the facts, arguing the toss on the evidence, listing what we have to give up and generally trying to change people's minds has got them only so far. Far more useful, we suggest, would be to follow the example of translating 'green' into a broader agenda. In the US the Sierra Club famously engaged the US Megachurch movement by translating 'conservation' into (the far more biblical) 'stewardship'.

Similarly, Google have tried to position their Chrome browser on the side of those building a better web, not arguing the toss with relative value of vs Explorer, Safari or whatever.

MAKE OTHER CHOICES SOCIAL PARIAHS

Social identity is often best expressed by In-groups and Out-groups and delineating one from the other. So while Pepsi spent the 1990s in the US, talking about being the 'choice of a new generation', the implied message was really 'Coke is your parents' and grandparents' drink'.

In the UK, Hobgoblin craft beer has challenged the weak-mindedness of the 'lagerboy' – although lager is still the standard tipple of the young British male.

Apple and Microsoft got into a fantastic battle with the latter's 'PC vs. Mac' marketing.

LINK TO OTHER CULTURAL PRACTICES

The Jamaican lager, Red Stripe, has a long history of supporting live music both at home and in export markets. Often long before it became the done thing for drinks brands – we've managed to trace a Red Stripe sponsorship back to 1964, for the emerging Ska music style (with instructions on how to dance to it…).

BE A BADGE OF BELONGING

Marketers have long enjoyed riding cultural waves but few are prepared to allow themselves to be adopted for major cultural movements. The VW Beetle became the de facto badge of the counterculture in the US, while Essigoni's Mini did the same for Swinging London.

MAKE PACKAGING A BADGE OF IDENTITY

Few packaging designs have real social identity. Coke's classic bottle shape is an exception. As Martin Lindstrom points out, it is unmistakeable, even when broken and denotes both product qualities and authenticity but more importantly the shared identity of Coke drinkers

Gateway computers used Friesian-patterned boxes to signal a different kind of computer was being delivered to a different kind of user – someone who clearly knows what's what.

Department stores like Selfridges and Bloomingdales have both created highly visible (and expensive) bags in order to use the fashion-set as walking endorsements of their brands.

COPYING PEERS: 'POPULARITY' STRATEGIES

POPULARITY

Finally, in the South-East quadrant, people are making their decisions based primarily on the choices of others but in a much less directed way than in the North-East: rather than following a few experts or accepted authorities, individuals will tend to work from their impressions of what most people happen to be doing or doing more. To COPY PEERS. In many decision contexts, this can mean a number of options are in with a chance of success.

This is a common decision style in markets in which there are many hard-to-distinguish options available, all of an acceptable quality. Patterns of choice tend to be quite volatile as sheer numbers of other people seem to be choosing an item at a particular time rather than anything inherent about the product or the person(s) being copied is what counts.

Strategies here are all rooted in POPULARITY (perceived or actual).

MEMBER GET MEMBER

...ARITY

SUPPORT THE THINGS THEY'RE ALREADY DOING TOGETHER

BE SEEN AS THE MOST POPULAR CHOICE

...ARITY

BE SEEN IN FAMOUS (BUT NOT EXPERT) HANDS

GIVE PEOPLE SOMETHING TO BRING THEM TOGETHER

POPULARITY

POPULARITY

RITUAL BEHAVIOUR

Heinz ketchup have encouraged tapping their bottle to get the product out. Magners
revol...

SEE ENTHUSIASM

Apple stores are temples to apple-man...
owner's ch...
fan gather...
do a simil...

VISIBLE CHOICES

Amazon is awash with other people's choices. You know when your neighbour has been to IKEA from the packaging on their doorstep.

BE SEEN AS THE POPULAR CHOICE

This is a surprisingly powerful strategy still, despite its abiding popularity. Whiskas cat food is still preferred by eight out of ten cats. Heinz beans used to claim that 'a million housewives every day' opened a tin of their beans. How can you calibrate your popularity?

HELP PEOPLE SEE EACH OTHER'S ENTHUSIASM

Apple stores are temples to Apple-mania. They're not great retail environments in the traditional sense but the layout is designed to give a platform for our enthusiasm for Apple and its products – clean, light and with lots of good sight-lines for us to see and hear other people playing with the latest devices.

Automotive owners' clubs are another great way to encourage this. In continental Europe, Mini owners' clubs regularly go on adventures together, just as motorbike fan boys and girls have always done 'rideouts' together.

Perhaps the best of these though are Lego's Brickfests, where the really hard core adult brick fans gather to build things and share their ideas and enthusiasm. This is now a compulsory part of the company's induction for new staff.

Makey Makey is 'an invention kit for the 21st Century', helping turn everyday objects into touchpads and combining them with the internet. All their marketing is rooted in showcasing what other people have done with the product.

MAKE OTHER PEOPLE'S CHOICES VISIBLE

While Amazon is awash with other people's choices and their thoughts and feedback – so much so it's hard to make sense of the sheer volume of reviews – perhaps its worthwhile thinking of other angles. For example, you know when your neighbour has been to IKEA from the packaging on the doorstep. How could you do the same?

BAKE IN VISIBILITY

It's hard to know what other people are doing unless you can see them doing it. Apple's iPod's white ear buds stood out at first against the black and the grey of other headphones. Magners' Irish cider pulled this trick by loading pint glasses meant for beer with ice (different and visible), thus requiring the branded bottle to be on the bar or table for twice as long as needed otherwise. Branded merchandise is just like this – what else are football 'colours'? The very pink branding of women's cancer charity events like the Moonwalk is another great example.

MAKE OTHER CHOICES SEEM LESS POPULAR

This is similar to the visibility point made earlier but it is rooted in managing perceptions of the choices of others. The best example of this is the UK tax authority's successful campaign to drive people to get their tax return in on time: 'Most people have already filed their tax return' is a great prompt. Encouraging fans of your football club to wear their 'colours' is an effective way to build your base by making other team choices less socially acceptable.

SUPPORT ACTIVITIES THAT PEOPLE ARE ALREADY DOING TOGETHER

It's much easier to lean into a group's existing behaviour or collective passion to borrow some perceived popularity than it is to persuade them to take up a new passion (you). That's why sponsoring already popular sports is so popular with marketers. That said, this sponsoring of sports people love is overcrowded and very expensive. Cancer Research UK did something very different – they observed many people not drinking in January and scaled it as 'Dryathlon'.

ENCOURAGE RITUAL BEHAVIOUR AROUND YOUR BRAND

Ritual behaviour is a shared, frequent and often highly visible signal of popularity. Brands and behaviours that can encourage this around way their choosers can take advantage of repeated signal of popularity.

Heinz ketchup have long encouraged (and amplified it in advertising) the tapping of their bottle to get the product out. Hendrick's Gin has encouraged a visually distinctive serve: putting a curl of cucumber in the glass.

GIVE PEOPLE THINGS TO DO (OR WATCH) TOGETHER

Fan gatherings are one thing but actually creating experiences around which people can interact is one step further. It's worth remembering that the world's greatest cycling event – the Tour de France – was originally invented by a newspaper to provide some exclusive content for readers (who may or may not have been interested in competitive cycling).

How do you engage a modern apolitical population? La Via Catalana was a 480 km human chain in support of Catalan independence from Spain, which was organized in September 2013, Catalonia's National Day. Some 1.6 million people took part in this high profile event, stretching from one border to the other, through 86 towns and cities.

A financial 'panic' can be seen to be spread in the same way as a virus but perhaps even more effectively because it gives people something to do together – panic, sell stocks, queue in line at the bank to withdraw their cash (as Brits did at the Northern Rock several years ago). This approach has become an effective working practice in reducing urban violence, for example, in CureViolence Chicago, a leading NGO in the US.

LIGHT LOTS OF FIRES

Sam Phillips, the founder of Sun Records, made millionaires of a handful of his artists – Johnny Cash, Elvis Presley, Carl Perkins and Jerry Lee Lewis (the so-called Millionaires Quartet). However, in order to be so successful in picking them, he had to also sign a whole bunch of others who – great voices aside – wouldn't be.

Google Labs does lots of interesting things that might lead to other things but they recognize that it's a numbers game, too. Most of these things will not work and somehow Google is OK with that.

You have to light lots of fires if popularity is the strategy.

MEMBER GET MEMBER

This is a classic recruitment strategy used by membership organizations.

Amex have built their business on it around the world over many years but more recently the giffgaff cell phone network used the same tactic, offering discounted tariffs for successful referrals, but you can also think about this in terms of user endorsement and peer-to-peer communication: the point is to ask your users to tell their friends. Sometimes you have to provide the tools to do so, but sometimes it's as simple as asking.

BE SEEN IN FAMOUS (BUT NOT EXPERT) HANDS

Many brands seek the halo of celebrity endorsement. George Clooney's association with Nespresso attracts attention and suggests popularity. James Bond's link with Aston Martin is a long-standing example from the movie business, and Range Rover have worked closely with Posh Spice to develop their new Evoke model and position it to a more urban female audience than might otherwise look to them. Beats by Dr Dre pulled a similar trick by giving elite athletes their headphones at the 2012 London Olympics and encouraging them to wear them in the stadium.

No marketer need ever feel short of things to copy: as this archive of pattern book strategies shows, the world is awash with examples of ways to solve problems just like the one you're wrestling with.

You just have to know where to look.

AND…once you know what kind of thing you're dealing with, the more confident you can be in narrowing down your search for appropriate examples. You don't have to just copy blindly.

But how will you get on in applying this to real world problems?

Let's see…

CONCLUSION

"Originality is for people with short memories."
—Grayson Perry

What this chapter covers:

Over to you: this chapter is about you putting what you've learned to work in strategizing around some real world problems.

To do better strategy – better, faster and richer.

To help you, I've included some of the answers we've come up with for these and similar problems but that's not in any way to suggest our solutions are definitive (far from it).

The point is for you to come up with your own answers – your own *better (or copied?)* solutions.

Using your skill, judgement, your amazing inherited talent for copying and the content of the previous chapter.

As Aristotle put it more than two millenia ago, "the things we have to learn before we can do them, we learn by doing them".

So let's get doing…

5 COPY BETTER

Applying what we've learned to real world problems

" The ultimate answer to life, the Universe and everything. "

To mathematicians, the number 42 is most unusual: it is a 'prionic' number (the product of two consecutive numbers, 6 × 7), an 'abundant' number (when you add together all of the whole numbers by which 42 is divisible, you get a number more than 42 itself). The number 42 is also a primary superperfect, a stormer, a harshad and self number, a Catalan number, a pentadecagonal and a meandric number. (Yes, this is all a bit beyond me, too.)

The number 42 seems to appear in all kinds of other places: in optics, 42 is the 'critical angle' (rounded to whole degrees) for which a rainbow appears. In computing, the password expiration policy for Microsoft Windows domain defaults at 42 days. In astronomy, the Orion Nebula is technically known as Messier object M42.

It has religious significance, too: in the Kabbalah, 42 is the number with which God creates the universe and the Babylonian Talmud contains a 42-lettered name of God. There are 42 principles of the Ancient Egyptian code of moral law (Ma'at) and 42 gods and goddesses depicted on the Day of Judgement in the Book of the Dead. The Gutenberg Bible is widely known by scholars as the 42-line Bible, as each page contains 42 lines.

Alice in Wonderland has 42 illustrations and the great baseball player, Jackie Robinson wore 42 on his jersey (he's now retired so it only gets worn in Major League Baseball on 15 April – Jackie Robinson Day when all players and officials wear it). There are 42 spots on a pair of standard dice and, of course, there are 42 Laws of Cricket. Also, 42 is the perfect score on the International Mathematical Olympiad and the maximum of core points to be awarded on the International Baccalaureate Diploma. And, of course, 42 is the number of months the Book of Revelation tells us that the Beast will hold dominion over the earth.

QUESTIONS VS. ANSWERS

For most of us though, 42 is probably best known as 'The answer to the ultimate question of life, the universe, and everything' in Douglas Adams' sci-fi masterpiece *The Hitchhiker's Guide to the Galaxy*. Adams suggests that it took an enormous supercomputer some 7.5 million years to crunch out this answer.

Unfortunately, as his narrator observes, no-one bothered to find out what the Ultimate Question was before the answer popped out from all that calculation. Knowing the answer is 42 is not much use; you'd need to know what the Ultimate Question was for it to be so. Which meant – according to Adams – building another really super, super supercomputer to work out the question to which 42 was the answer.

I think questions are way more useful than answers, which is why this final chapter is going to help you get good at tackling different kinds of strategy problems by working with the three core questions which we've raised during the course of this book:

- What kind of thing is this?
- What kind of solutions are appropriate?
- What would that look like?

Don't worry – despite the numerical brain-twisting this chapter has opened with – this will be practical rather than a theoretical read. The point being not to be absolutely right with your answers but to learn how to ask yourself the questions.

However, before we leap into the first example, let's just spend a while reviewing the very simple process based on the three central questions.

1. WHAT KINDA THING

'What kinda?' questions are very practical: if your boiler breaks down, you don't want the engineer to just know about this boiler – or about your house – but how boilers generally work and how they don't coupled with a wide-ranging experience of different houses, different plumbing set-ups and what can happen when you try to fix them.

> ## 'What kinda?' questions are very practical.

If your car starts making a weird noise, the garage mechanic doesn't want to know if it's a C-sharp or a B-flat. Or that it goes beep-beeeeeep-bip rather than beep-bip-bip (although with some computers this kind of error message can provide a precise diagnosis of the problem). For most mechanics it's the kind of sound that matters and what that might mean in different situations in different cars (and not just yours).

If you want to stop a population doing something or get them to start doing something else, it's always better to have a firm grip on 'what kinda thing' you're dealing with. What kind of behaviour is it? What other behaviours are like it? What other behaviours could you learn from?

ELEPHANT TRAPS

One of the ideas behind this book is that the way you approach strategy is as important as the strategy tools or skills you have or deploy. Too often strategy is just something you do – you just leap in and get strategizing. We treat the practice as if it is 'ideology-light' as some of my more committed political friends would put it. But as with any form of human behaviour, the practice of strategy has assumptions built in as default settings and these hidden assumptions can lead any of us astray.

Here are two kinds of trap that strategists fall into by doing this rather than challenging their assumptions about how they do what they do: what the golfers might call 'my favourite club' and our old friend, 'singularity'.

'My favourite club' is a common enough fault amongst amateurs of the game: rather than really examine the challenge of the course in front of you (and work out what the appropriate approaches might be), you find yourself reaching for that thing that you always do, that trusty 5 iron or whatever. There's a temptation to do this in fishing circles, too – I've got two or three go-to trout flies that I always use, almost without thinking because they've always seemed to catch me fish in the past. I don't feel quite as confident without them.

In strategy, this means just approaching problem solving in the way you've always done ('because that's what doing strategy in my field is'). We see a lot of this in marketing and policy circles. Educationalists like testing and early interventions. Marketers like 'more impact' and 'revolutionary new approaches' (sometimes).

> ❝ **Beware the tyranny of the singular – you will never have perfect knowledge of the 'initial conditions' of any one case.** ❞

The other trap for the strategist is to get lost in the detail of the specific case – the tyranny of the singular. This is because we strategists assume that each problem we face is a unique and different thing: only by describing the singularity in great detail could anyone hope to develop an appropriate response. Modern technology seems to play to this – giving us more and more data points and more things to measure. And with it, more noise and less signal, as Nassim Taleb has pointed out.[57] Also, of course, much slower response times. This is all too common in both marketing, management and policy circles.

Of course, it's going to be good to understand the specifics of the particular case but in the real world, this kind of event-specific understanding is very often not available at the time but only possible long after the fact, when the dust (and fires) have settled. For example, *The Guardian* LSE in-depth study of the 2011 London riots, based on the methodology used for the post-mortem of the 1957 Chicago riots, would have been no use if you were advising a police chief or politician as London burned.

In most other cases – whether it's dealing with the fallout on social media of a service outage or in launching a new product into a competitive market – you will need a working understanding of *what kind of thing* you're dealing with; the perfect analysis of hindsight is never going to be relevant to you. You will never have perfect knowledge, a perfect grasp of what scientists call 'the initial conditions' of a phenomenon, so get over it!

So where are you going to get this working understanding? From asking 'what kinda?' questions again. From putting this instance of a thing in the context of other instances. From looking back over time, across categories and across national borders.

2. WHAT KIND OF STRATEGY?

Once you've got a handle on the kind of behaviour you're dealing with, very quickly you'll know what kind(s) of successful strategy to choose. Or, at least, where in the pattern books (Chapter 4) you need to rummage.

You could just spin the wheel and copy what look likes success or what someone you respect might choose. This is after all what often happens in the real world: consider, for example, phenomena like the rush in marketing circles a decade ago to build loyalty or CRM programmes; or, more recently, to get a social media strategy or a Facebook page or some world-class text analytics capability. They certainly didn't happen because of considered decision making but rather by copying successful businesses and following the hype.

It's not that I think this way of seeking solutions is always going to be wrong – clearly lots of people have had success in the past using this approach (although most have not). The thing is this: without asking 'what kinda' questions like 'what kind of problem are we facing?', you're picking blind: rolling the dice.

Each of the strategies described in our pattern books has been allocated to that book (a) because it's demonstrably successful somewhere else and (b) because it's demonstrably successful for that kind of thing. So rather than rush to

answers, ask yourself 'what kind of thing will solve this kind of problem?'

Don't focus on trying to find the perfect singular answer – take three, four or five that seem to make sense and work with them. This will stop the perfectionist inside you taking over. And the single white female copycat.

3. WHAT DOES THAT LOOK LIKE?

In Chapter 2, we made a big deal about copying well (as opposed to badly) – loosely not tightly. This chapter really helps put that to work.

- First, copy from far away – from examples that are not from your immediate market or context.
- Second, copy a number of things, rather than look for the perfect singular one – there are always going to be other ways of solving a problem than the one you land on first, so sorting 15–20 possible strategies is always better (and faster) than trying to isolate that one perfect strategy.
- Third (and perhaps most important), ensure you add variation in the way you copy. This means moving away from the abstract and the conceptual answers to 'what kind of solution' to real and concrete versions. Most people find this easy to do – certainly much easier than coming up with a spanking new idea themselves (this is the difference between innovation and invention, right here). Draw it, write it, show it – sing it, if you like!

We always encourage very practical rather than very conceptual answers to this final question: what would it look like? What would it feel like? What would a customer experience? Why would it be fun? Remembering, of course, that this is just a first rough version, rather than a finished piece.

A good test here is this: what could you make that showed the idea to your boss without having to explain the concept?

Innovator Kim Erwin calls this a:

> *'build to think prototype':*[58] *giving other people 'just enough experience to imagine the concept, without distracting detail and quality craftsmanship that signal a more developed idea… not to be pretty or complete or accurate but to help the team learn, experiment, and develop unfinished ideas using tangible objects'.*

The kind of thing you can get instant feedback on. 'Credible but sketchy' as Heather Reavy puts it.[59]

The extraordinary success of animation house Pixar Studios is at least partly built on creating this kind of rough and ready 'build to think' prototype[60] for each and every idea the team has: rough films ('reels') are created from storyboards to help show the story the director wants to make, to explore the reality of telling a particular story and thus get feedback from the directors, mentors and peers in the company (the Pixar Brainstrust). As CEO Ed Catmull notes,[61] without working this way, the multi-million dollar *Up* would have ended up being a movie about a castle in the sky, two princes who hated each other and their life-and-death struggle to get back to the clouds to claim the kingdom for their own.

Turn your strategy into something – a thing that I can respond to (rather than a concept board or document).

UP NEXT

What follows now is a series of real world challenges to apply your three questions to.

As much as you can, please try to work through the examples (don't just skip to what we came up with) as if you were trying to solve them for real.

But as you do so, remember it isn't the answers that matter so much as how you apply the questions.

Bonne chance! Hals- und Beinbruch! Good luck!

Challenge 1: Mygizmo

The brief: You have to launch a new product into an existing category – say a kind of consumer electronics.

What's your go-to-market strategy?

Many professionals considering this kind of challenge will default to what they've done before – to the media choices and the tactics they have found useful previously.

Or to the default settings of the category or industry: what do other businesses do in this market? What are the rules of this particular game?

Or, to that approach that [insert your most admired brand here] used last year for that successful launch of theirs.

In seeking a better answer than this (and sometimes, let's be honest, as a preparation for justification for some more outlandish strategy we've wanted to do for a while) many people just dig: deeper into the specific characteristics of the case they go, hoping to identify some unique insight into the audience or some unique way of describing the product or some unique proposition that nobody has found before.

A unique answer to this unique problem.

Well, you could go that way but let's try asking some 'what kinda' questions instead.

What kinda behaviour?

Again take your pen and paper out and draw yourself the sorting box, so:

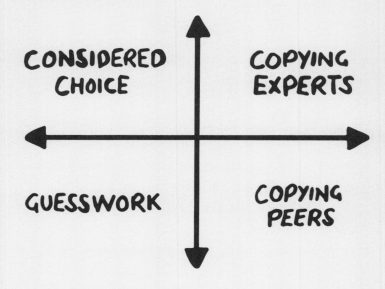

Think now about what you know about how people buy in this category. What kind of choice is it?

Do people buy based on a detailed consideration of the utilities of a handful of options (North-West) or do they just buy what seems most salient because all the options are the same (South-West)? Do they look to other people – a few expert voices or authorities (North-East) – or is it just the sense of what's popular that they use to make decisions (South-East)?

THAT UNHELPFUL 'THING' THING

Manufacturing companies tend to assume that individuals choose between their products in this way – the way that classical economics teaches (and that they tell themselves they do, also). That is, by comparing the utilities and costs of the different options in front of them. Making their own minds up on the basis of the quality of things (much like they imagine they do themselves – 'I'm not the kind of guy who gets fooled by all this marketing fluff …', 'I'm not affected by advertising').

Of course, this plays really well in many manufacturing businesses because it pays all due respect to the part of the organization which still calls the tunes – the factory and its (highly rational) engineering workforce. Even in over-supplied commoditized markets (have you tried to buy a TV set recently? Line after line of (big, bigger and enormous) thin black boxes with complex TM'd features that even the salesperson struggles to grasp let alone articulate).

While healthcare professionals and policy makers don't always deal so obviously in factory-made Things, they also think like this. Being experts, they know what you should do and presume that telling you what to do and why you should do it. If only they could get you to listen and pay attention and do what they say.

If you ever hear a meeting discuss the need to 'educate' an audience, this is a big signal that the conversation presumes seeing the Thing and appreciation of the Thing as the key to unlock the targeted behaviour change. Ditto politicians – 'we're not getting our message across' is a good marker that they imagine this is how voters make their choices.

> **Think really carefully about how people actually come to buy this kind of thing.**

It's a version of what's called an 'information-deficit' communication model. That is, that information will change things – information about the product, the desired behaviour or the option in a voting booth. Which might be the most appropriate model to think through the problem in front of you but is almost certainly not.

Manufacturing businesses like megapixels and frames-per-second and 'crystal-clear colour' and the like. But does the consumer?

> **Check your assumptions again.**

REALITY CHECK

If this default setting were right, it would put the decision style clearly in the North-West corner – in Considered Choice.

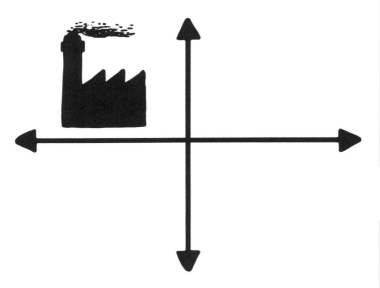

But is this how real people actually choose? Is this really how people buy or have ever bought electrical appliances?

At this point you may be feeling the draw of a particular part of the map: if you're a WoM fan, you'll be looking to your favourite North-East quadrant with its handful of influential individuals; if you're a Nudge fan, you'll find yourself drawn more to the South-West – where individual cognitive biases dominate. Try to resist this temptation – for now.

East or West?

Let's start by considering whether the way buyers choose this kind of thing is based on independent decisions or are the decisions of others key to shaping individual choices? In other words, is the category on the Western or the Eastern side of our sorting map.

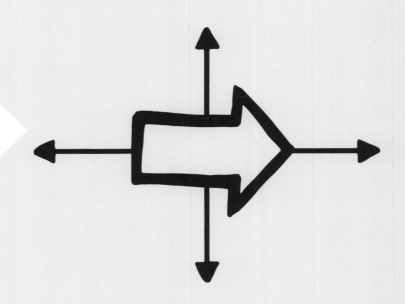

Perhaps you might ask whether or not recommendation is particularly popular in the market:

- Is Amazon full of reviews of products?
- Is there a trade press with expert opinion at its heart?
- Are there online communities discussing the products, their virtues and vices and people's experience with them?
- Is the choice of this kind of thing visible to other people – at the point of purchase or otherwise?
- Is it embedded in other cultural traditions?
- Does it involve or evoke social status or social identity?

Any of these will tend to suggest that category is chosen socially (on the Eastern side of the map).

In fact, in most consumer electronics categories – from cameras to laptops – this is the kind of thing you'll see a lot of. So if you find yourself moving this way, the next question becomes whether or not you are dealing with Copying Experts (North-East) or Copying Peers (South-East).

A simple way to resolve this is to examine whether there are a small group of experts or authorities that individuals tend to follow (NB not just that there are a bunch of noisy self-appointed experts pumping out their opinions to the world: the important thing is whether individuals defer to them).

> **❝Is there a small group of experts or authorities that individuals tend to follow?❞**

Another is to consider how important a badge owning or using the product is – what it says to consumers and their peers about themselves? Do fads and fashions come and go over time or are patterns of behaviour stable over the long run? And are they central to abiding group identities?

If the answer to the former of these questions is yes, you're more likely than not dealing with the North-East. If no, or if you get a positive answer to the second and third question, then you're likely to be dealing with a predominantly South-East choice style.

Two kinds of thing?

Let's say you conclude that the reality of how people choose in this category turns out to be based on copying experts and authority figures (i.e. in the North-East). This is after all how classic Bass diffusions are supposed to work – the product may or may not be superior but you learn about it from expert peers.

This is in stark contrast to how we suspect the client thinks about it – remember most manufacturing and engineering businesses imagine that people choose based on the product's inherent qualities and its clever features and utilities (i.e. in the North-West).

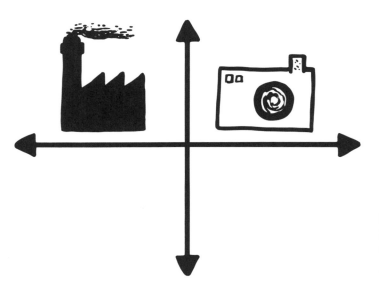

What kinda strategy?

If true, this is an important finding: it suggests there is a real opportunity to enhance the clients' efforts to get people to buy Mygizmo simply by deploying strategies that match the reality of how people really choose in the category. This is an open goal for you, the strategist.

So, rather than simply focus on strategies from the Better bucket, this analysis points to consideration of strategies from the Expert bucket. Let's compare some examples from each:

BETTER	EXPERT
Build a demonstrably better mousetrap	*Make advocates of expert users*
Use high price to signal better	*Give people something to do together*
Restrict supply to emphasize better	*Find social structures to support*
Give the product away to demo better	*Find expert makers to endorse Mygizmo*
Create a new torture test of better	*Be a badge of belonging*
Quantify better	*Link to social identities*
Guarantee satisfaction	*Link to other cultural practices*

Of course, this shift in focus would also have a big influence on the mix of communications tools and channels.

On the Better side, more traditional communications thinking would predominate: you'd be thinking about channels down which you send messages to individual buyers. The point is getting members of your audience to appreciate Better.

On the Expert side, you'd be thinking less about media as 'channels' for your messages and more about helping Expert recommendation and preference be seen and heard by your audience.

This is not to say that you won't be using traditional tools but certainly the newer social platforms would be more prominent in your mix than previously.

> ## " Matching the kind of strategy to how people choose has got to be a good thing. "

Show me

Once you've identified strategies and examples:

- What would that look like in my market?
- What would you do if you were to copy it across into your marketing plans?

Don't try to edit or evaluate yet – just copy and turn into a simple conceptual prototype.

- Turn the strategy example you've borrowed from 'Find expert makers to endorse Mygizmo' into a hypothetical version such as 'Recruit NASA's chief scientist to be your Dr Dre.
- Turn 'Give people something to do together' into 'create secret events at SXSW for all Mygizmo early adopters'.
- Turn 'Find social structures or identities to support' into 'Target the maker community who are not embraced by big tech companies' or [in the US] work with church groups who might spread your idea for you.
- And so on.

The important thing here is to (a) copy, (b) copy from a distance, (c) copy many things, (d) add variety as you copy and make it real when you do so (as Chapter 2 discussed).

Suddenly, from no strategies you have a real focus and half a dozen things that are worth market-testing with a small number of prospects.

Challenge 2: Render unto Caesar

Here's a rather different challenge from the public policy playbook:

How do you get people to file their tax return on time?

Millions of Americans are late filing and the same is true in the UK, too. To be honest, I have been known to slip up this way, myself.

For all tax authorities, late filing is more than some mere administrative problem: it costs the government a fortune in delayed tax receipts (they too have a cashflow balance to consider) and it is often the first indicator of full non-payment. Governments don't like late filing or late payment either way – they need the money and the confidence that the money will be forthcoming.

Both the US and UK tax authorities use a range of threats and punishments to encourage the laggards. But for all the tax authorities' efforts, many of us still resist, never quite getting round to submitting our paperwork.

What additional ideas can you suggest to help the taxman?

Show me the money

The first task again is to ask 'what kinda?' questions: What kind of decision are we targeting? Why do those who don't file fail their returns on time do so? Is this based on a considered choice? Is it rational or emotionally-led?

Perhaps people aren't aware of the fines and other penalties that kick in immediately the filing is late. This is possible for many but the tax authorities in both countries have long advertised the deadlines (which don't tend to change from year to year) and the fines. Equally, there are lots of financial and tax advisors particularly in the US shouting about the deadlines as they loom and the penalties and punishments. It might still be worth testing what happens when you up the volume on this strategy.

But why do some people still not file on time?

Maybe the key to unlocking the behaviour of these non-filers is the insight the behavioural economists have brought us: that much of financial decision making is in the South – rather than in the North-West of our map. To be honest, humans and considered

Doing the math

My old friend, Alex Batchelor tells a great story about challenging an audience of professional accountants on their own unwillingness to 'do the math': first, he asked them which of them could calculate depreciating values of capital assets. Most raised their hands to show that, yes, as financial professionals, they could do the basics. Then, he asked the room to keep their hands raised if they'd bought a new car in the previous few years. Again a forest of hands remained raised, perhaps proud of all the professional success it indicated. And then the killer punch: 'how many of you used the skill with numbers to do that calculation when you chose your car?' Silence – only a few hands remained aloft.

This is true, for even the smartest and most numerate amongst us. Indeed, a really important foundation piece of work by Nobel Laureate, Daniel Kahnemann and his research partner Amos Twersky in what we now call 'Behavioural Economics' demonstrated that medical professionals are just as poor as their patients in calculating outcomes and probabilities (not better as you'd expect trained and numerate scientists to be).

Most of us, most of the time, don't use our noodles nearly as much as we think we do (or tell ourselves we do). Kahnemann and co describe 2 systems of thinking in our brains: System 1, all intuitive and approximate, using shorthands – heuristics – and rules of thumb; System 2, rational and considered and logical. While most of us would like to believe System 2 ruled our lives, it's System 1 that helps us get through the day and thrive as we do in complex and uncertain environments. It's fast, effective and – while it leaves us prone to the many errors the psychologists and self-help book authors love – it's incredibly efficient.

financial services decisions rarely go well together. We don't often 'do the math', even if we can (this was one of the prime findings of pioneering behavioural economist Daniel Kahneman's research into patients' and medical professionals' decision making). 'Doing the math' is definitely in the North-West.

That's why most of us get stuck with a bad deal on travel insurance or on our personal banking account or our energy bills: we avoid having to do any thinking about the numbers.

The power of inertia

Another aspect that many financial service businesses exploit is our inertia – our unwillingness to re-examine bad deals, even when we are prompted to do so by term-contracts. The UK government have made strenuous efforts in recent years to force banks and energy providers to make it as easy as possible to move but still they struggle to rouse us, even with 100% price rises over the last decade: 75% of UK households are currently on a standard energy tariff which costs significantly more than the cheapest available. Even in Q4 2013, when the Labour Party Leader Ed Milliband sparked a huge media storm over energy prices, less than 2% of UK households switched their supplier.

Habit or inertia or guesswork, whatever you call it, financial decisions are more often than not in the South-West.

So what kinds of strategy might we use for the taxman?

Suggested South West strategies

Shout louder

Make it hard to choose alternatives

Make it easier to choose your option

Incentivize the desired behaviour

Shout louder

This is what policy people often suggest: raise awareness of the details and then let individuals make their own choices. Not entirely wrong but how loud do you have to shout to make much of a difference? When do you reach the point of diminishing returns?

Make it hard to choose to file late by emphasizing the negatives

Politicians like this kind of solution and it often plays well to the crowds: hike up the punishments and disincentives for filing late. Again not necessarily wrong but there are normally diminishing returns to be had here, too.

Incentivize early filing

Steal from 'factoring' practices: give cash discounts for filing (e.g. three months) early (NB as in commercial businesses, you need to be careful that you are not just giving money away to people who would have paid full price on time with this kind of promotion).

Make it easier to file earlier

One way we might do this might be to resend the previous year's return and suggest that the numbers will be assumed to be the same if they are not amended.

Another might be to simplify the return form – reduce its complexity or accept estimates rather than detail.

Incentivize those who file early by focusing on the emotional benefit for filing early

Remind later filers from previous years how much better they will feel. Get individuals to write themselves a letter/email from last year, which you can then send them in the run-up to the following year's deadline.

Moving beyond the South-West strategies

Above and beyond all the excellent experiments which the UK Government's Behavioural Insights Team have conducted over the last three years, this particular fiscal problem has provided some of their best learning.[62]

In particular, the use of a South-East 'social proof' strategy seems to have outperformed all others: a letter which leads with thoughts such as 'nine out of ten people have already filed – why not you?' gets a significantly better response than others.

Why might this be? At the simplest level, it suggests that while the targeted behaviour may currently be being shaped by individuals choosing on their own, given the chance they will follow what those around them are doing.

Given what we know about the (un)suitability of the human mind to financial decision making, this would make a lot of sense. And also the resistance to the more North-West strategies that policy makers lean towards (explain the benefits or disbenefits of filing on time or late).

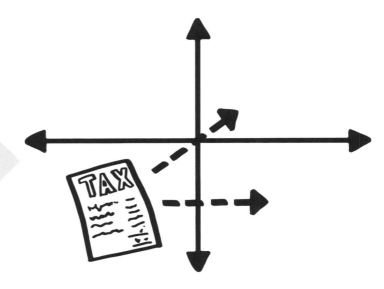

If this is the case, are there other kinds of social strategy you can deploy? Here are some suggestions from both South-East and North-East that might help:

EXPERTISE/AUTHORITY	POPULARITY
Give people something to do together In the US, Intuit have started encouraging tax filing parties for certain demographics. Could something like this work for you?	**Popularize ritual behaviour** Is there a gesture that you can encourage people to do when they've filed? A 'completion' fist-bump?
Be a badge of belonging Can you make the display of 'I've filed on time' a badge of honour for certain groups? On line or in their community media?	**Bake in visibility** How can you make on-time filing visible? Is there some sign you can get people to display?
Link to other cultural practices Are there church or other groups who might provide a credible channel for your message? Can you build or hack a platform for further mutual influence?	**Support things they're already doing together** Are there sports or activity clubs that meet just before the deadline? Can you support these?
Get experts to advocate Are their business or entrepreneurial figures to whom your audience defer? At a national or local level?	**Be seen in famous hands** Is there a celebrity who might reach your demographic with an 'I just filed' message?
Etc.	**Make non-filing less popular** What are the numbers? Does 1 in 10 seem small enough?

What would you do?

Go back to the Eastern pattern books and see what else you can make.

Challenge 3: When social is the problem

In these first two examples, *social* strategies (from the Eastern part of the map) have proved to be key to shifting the targeted behaviour.

However, in many other cases, it is social decision-making styles that make the targeted behaviour hard to shift. Lots of choices are either embedded deep in cultural identities or attached to other strongly social behaviours or they raise tricky questions about how one individual relates to another.

Take, for example, hand-washing (or 'sanitizing'as the US Center for Disease Control puts it):

> *Clean hands prevent infections. Keeping hands clean prevents illness at home, at school, and at work. Hand hygiene practices are key prevention measures in healthcare settings, in daycare facilities, in schools and public institutions, and for the safety of our food.'*

However, it's much harder than one might think to get people to do it.

Even amongst those who should know better – the medical professionals – it has proved very difficult to achieve high levels of compliance (and not just in British Hospitals!), whatever the educational input. Winning the argument – stating the facts, whether baldly or emotively – doesn't seem to change the behaviour enough or do so sustainably. Why might this resistance be so strong?

Part of the issue here is the habitual nature of the behaviour, reinforced over many years but it's also true that the fact that these kinds of behaviours are often private or associated with private choices (hand-washing and the bathroom being an obvious thing). Hand-washing outside of these locations perhaps seems unnecessary and thus a signal of other things (for example, neurosis or distrust). What's missing is a sense that this is what everyone else does.

If this were the case, then the indicated strategies might be best sourced from the South-East and popularity: you might choose to place hand-washing and cleaning facilities in public places (in high traffic sites and in full view of patients). You might oversupply dispensers in public places to create again a sense of popularity. And so on.

Very often the differences between how different groups of people respond in different ways reveals some North-Eastern (cultural) forces at work. Take for example, this picture.

To you and I, this image of the boy with a baguette may seem charmingly French but, as my friend Andrew Missingham points out, to a West African (and maybe to many an American) this seems terribly unhygienic. Putting unwrapped food in one of the hottest, sweatiest parts of your body seems just asking for trouble in terms of food hygiene.

At the same time, the different associations the word 'sanitize' evokes in listeners in different Anglophone cultures is striking and suggests there are other big cultural factors at play in shaping the status quo (i.e. North-East).

The Little Parisian Boy, Paris, France, 1952
Source: Succession Willy RONIS/Diffusion Agence Gamma-Rapho/Masters/Getty Images

In the US *sanitize* is about clean and safe and without hostile germs; in the UK and in other parts of Europe, *sanitize* is about removing naturally occurring stuff. Sanitize says a lot of what I think about you (unclean) and therefore what you think about me (you can rarely escape such stuff in English culture). Frankly, the American obsession with hand-wipes and gels comes across to many Brits as little short of neurosis. To some (OCD-type) personalities over here, hand-sanitizing is readily embraced but for many it is profoundly alien.

149

HOW TO UNLOCK CULTURALLY ENTRENCHED BEHAVIOUR

If this is the kind of thing you discover to be the case, you're going to need more than popularity strategies to drive adoption of the behaviour in an English organization: you're also going to need to harness some North-Eastern strategies to counter the strong cultural bias against hand-washing.

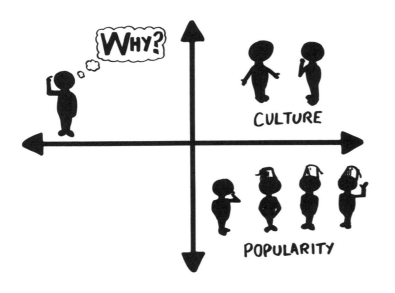

So what kinds of strategies might we use?

Suggested North East strategies

Give people something to do together

Make packaging a badge

Find social structures and identities to support

Make advocates of expert users and authorities

Here are some of the ideas which appealed to me (and the strategies they are based on):

Give people something to do together

Why not encourage the creation of rituals of hand-washing – at the beginning and ends of meetings and consultations? Something that both parties do together to start or end the conversation. Maybe disguise the hand element by focusing on wiping down surfaces initially (desk- and table-wipes as opposed to hand-wipes).

Make packaging a badge

Rather than present hand-washing and sanitizing products in formats which suggest medical, health or bathroom concerns (as is currently the case), why not present them in high status formats – the equivalent of the silver cigarette case. This would also have the effect of creating a 'social object' – something around which individuals can interact. Limit their free use to high status individuals initially – mission-critical teams, perhaps.

Find social structures and identities to support

Why not create a sense of competition between different departments – reporting their usage of hand washing materials to each other (with or without linking this to sick-days or business performance). Similar strategies have been deployed in hotels to drive up the rates of bedding/laundry reuse.

Make advocates of expert users and authorities

Identify those individuals to whom others in the organization defer – for example, the best salesperson or the best surgeon – and get them to advocate for the practice.

The role of culture and social choices in keeping things as they are is more common than you might think.

- Why is the US a hard liquor country when the UK is predominantly a beer-drinking culture on the shift to being a wine-drinking country? Culture.
- Why are parenting styles hard to change? Culture.
- Why do practices like female genital mutilation continue, despite the educational efforts? Culture.
- Why do Scandinavians (and MidWesterners) have to take their midday and evening meals so early? Culture.
- Why do British politicians have to resign over sexual affairs and French ones not? Culture.
- Why does the clientele of an American diner expect unlimited refills of their coffee cup when Italians don't? Culture.
- Why can Colombian pilots – as Malcolm Gladwell observes in *Outliers* – not tell each other (and NYC's ball-breaking) Air Traffic Controllers that they're out of fuel? Culture.
- Why does American Leadership style not work everywhere?[63] Culture.

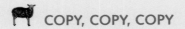

WHAT HAVE WE LEARNED SO FAR?

I hope that exploring on these few examples has given you rather more confidence in working with the four-box map and the pattern books of strategy.

In the *first challenge* (Mygizmo) we merely demonstrated the value of getting a better answer to the first of these *kinda* questions right: challenging the assumptions about the targeted behaviour opens up a whole raft of more appropriate – and more effective – strategies to test. And does so quickly.

In the *second* (tax returns) I tried to push further by encouraging you to disentangle a false assumption about financial decisions that experts in this market hold dear – the notion that people do or should have to think about what they do in finance (North-West). Once this is unpicked, other – more social – strategies come to the surface and the solutions are relatively quick to get to.

In the *third challenge* (when social is the problem), I encouraged you to question how the status quo is shaped and to see the need to unpick North-Eastern factors which act on barriers that prevent behaviour change.

The key thing to remember here is to ask more *kinda* questions

- What kind of thing is this?
- What kind of strategies might work to address that?
- What would each look like?

The final example is one which may seem a long way from home for many of us, but it shows how the COPY, COPY, COPY approach can help to develop strategies and solutions for even the most unusual challenges.

Let's go!

The Final Challenge: Out on the streets

'At the end of April, the eyes of the world were on London as a dashing prince and a radiant princess, William and Kate, rode in a horse-drawn carriage through streets lined with cheering crowds... four months later, the world [is] watching London again as hooded youths ran riot.'

Chief Rabbi, Jonathan Sacks[64]

It is 5 August 2011. London and other major UK cities have been caught in a forest fire of violence and looting: youngsters are roaming the streets and police have been caught short of manpower and logistical back up. The media is dominated by one story – the apocalyptic vision of urban dystopia that is happening right outside.

Imagine you are the one person to whom everyone else is looking – the strategist for the Prime Minister.

What should he/she do or not do to deal with the unprecedented chaos on the streets? All the other advisors will be tempted to reach for their favourite policy responses. You alone have the chance to think clearly and independently. Where do you think the government should start in its response?

Before we start, write down the first three strategies that come into your head. And why? Don't dwell on this too long.

Strategy 1

Strategy 2

Strategy 3

153

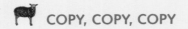

What kinda thing?

As with every other example you'll come across – both here and in the real world – job number one is to characterize the behaviour behind the phenomenon you are studying: What kind of thing is this?

The spark that lit the fires seems to have been the shooting of a Tottenham man, Mark Duggan, by Metropolitan Police marksmen and in particular the subsequent seemingly unconcerned and unhelpful treatment of his family and friends' complaints. Within a matter of hours, youth across the borough were burning cars, smashing windows and fighting with the police officers sent to disperse them.

> **Something genuinely disruptive was happening...A Revolution, maybe?**

As the days spun by – as Saturday turned to Sunday and Sunday to Monday and on into the working week – the rioters themselves turned to looting (TVs and trainers seemed to be a popular choice although one unfortunate individual was later jailed for stealing a bottle of water). The chaos rapidly raced not just through London but to the suburbs and centres of other English cities – to Birmingham, Liverpool and Manchester.

For a while, it seemed that something genuinely disruptive was happening – the kind of self-organizing mass action that is depicted in Hollywood's classic dystopian adventure movies, in the violent console games that explore post-apocalyptic cityscapes with trails of murder and chaos or indeed in the fevered dreams of any would-be urban revolutionary. An Uprising. *A Revolution, maybe?*

In the face of this, many of London's law-abiding office and shop workers left their place of work early, keen to avoid getting caught up in mad and bad things unspecified; water-cooler conversations being dominated by scary stories of crazed mobs and uncontrollable wickedness from the night before. Of secret messages sent and received on new-fangled social media platforms. And – of course – of narrow escapes and living to tell the tale.

Now think

What does this tell you about 'what kind of behaviour' you're dealing with?

Draw yourself a pair of axes as before.

Where do you map the riots? Is it in the North, the South, the East or the West?

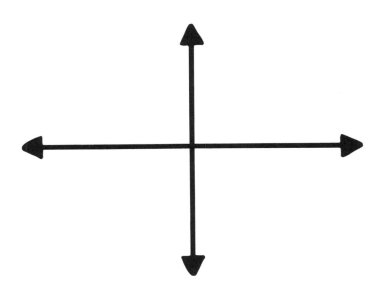

What kinda thing, Prime Minister?

Politicians and media commentators tend to go straight in with what seems to be the self-evident truth of a situation, often based on questionable assumptions and 'common sense'. So it's worth noting what those assumptions are before we go any further.

For example, the British Prime Minister, David Cameron, managed to grab hold of two very popular default responses to the outbreak of rioting, at his first appearance in front of a very packed recalled Houses of Commons during the riots on 11 August. Interestingly, the mainstream media were ready to join in on the chorus and echo his assertions.

Tough times, bad people

On the one hand, he deployed a largely North-West analysis.

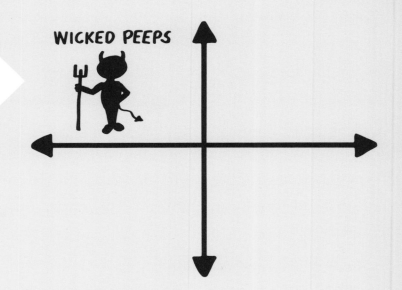

According to this line of thinking, the riots are to be understood as primarily the product of individual pathologies – of sick or just plain wicked individuals who have chosen to commit various crimes. Which of course leads straight to an easy fix: these individuals need to be punished to teach them not to do it again; they need to be taught how to behave.

Prime Minister Cameron's speech in the specially recalled House of Commons was rooted in this line of analysis.

'You will pay for what you have done. We will track you down, we will find you, we will charge you and we will punish you.'

(C/o C4 News online.)

The Mayor of London took a similar line in subsequent interviews:

'[we] need to ensure that all those convicted of charges [arising from the riots] ... are made to face up to the enormity of their appalling conduct and the impact that it has had on their community ... [they] should be held to account for their behaviour and the capital will feel badly let down if the punishment available to the courts does not support this objective ...'

All very (North-)Western: individuals were acting independently, either through faulty morals or a poor miscalculation of the utility of that course of action. Tell (or flog!) them not to do it! They'll come to their senses soon enough.

Those who take this line often want to exclude any other causes – wickedness/sickness is what it is, plain and simple. The *Daily Mail* was particularly keen to avoid any confusion with other (political) causes: 'to blame [other factors e.g.] the cuts is immoral and cynical – this is criminality plain and simple'.[65]

❝ This is criminality plain and simple. ❞

Broken society

At the same time, the Prime Minister embraced a rather more North-Eastern line of analysis as he bemoaned a crumbling of the social order and the failure of experts and authorities to hold things together.

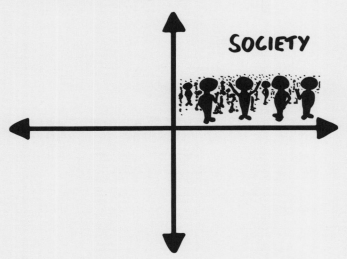

Not just sick individuals but a sick society which needed rebuilding.

> 'The sight of those young people running down streets smashing windows, taking property, looting, laughing as they go – the problem with that is a complete lack of responsibility, a lack of proper parenting, a lack of proper upbringing, a lack of proper ethics, a lack of proper morals. That is what we need to change.'

158

To observers of Mr Cameron, this is clearly a version of his well-rehearsed theme of 'broken society': his own moral crusade on behalf of the traditional British way of life. (Subsequently, his speeches again referred to the 'moral collapse' that the riots either portended or represented. Either way, seemed determined to reverse the decline in the way we live. Whether it be through reviewing all policies affecting the 120,000 most 'troubled' families or a newly announced 'war on gangs').

To many this is a strangely comforting analysis: it presents the targeted behaviour at a scale that is understandable – the enclosed community or village – and highlights the importance of the social and ethical responsibilities of all those in that community. The Miss Marple scale, you might call it:

> 'Well, my dear…human nature is much the same everywhere, and, of course, one has opportunities of observing it at closer quarters in a village.'[66]

All of which may play well with many voters but what help does it give you in stopping the riots rolling around London like so many thunderclaps? What can you do in the short-term with this line of thinking?

A related North Easterly point of view sees things on an altogether different scale: here, the riots are understood as the product of an entire large-scale social system – the result of the complex interplay of abiding social, cultural and economic factors (rather than in terms of the actions of individual rioters). In other words, a North-Eastern problem but one in which the focus is on higher-level forces that cause the rioters to act as they do.

This is not necessarily any lazy soft-left perspective. Social reformers from as far back as Charles Dickens have seen crime and civic disruption in this way, as the *inevitable product of poverty and social and economic deprivation*. The poor cannot help but be so, they argue. The poor can do no other, so the thinking goes. They just act in ways that they are forced by the world to act. "Society is to blame" as the old saw has it. And the poor merely pawns. They are at the bottom of the pile: the social, culturally, politically and economically disaffected and they deserve our sympathy rather than our scorn.

❝ We Brits have long bemoaned the decline in social order. ❞

Which interpretation may indeed be valid from the lofty perspective of the social reformer but it can lead to some odd conclusions: part of the answer it seems is that we need to give to the voiceless as one social worker wrote in *The Guardian*.[67] 'The young rioters are the experts of their own experience and the only way we can begin to recover from the riots is by listening to the reality of the problem.' A good dose of listening?

The real problem with this line of analysis is that it points to very little that we can do to address the immediate situation – handwringing and hot tea aside. To the policy maker surrounded by TV broadcasts of cars on fire and running battles between police and youth and of course 'questions in the House', what

can you do with this large scale model of social change to impact on the behaviour you see around you? *It may be true, but is it useful? How do you engage with human pawns?*

Of course on the most expedient level, it also fails to give the boss, the PM, the sense or the appearance of being in control – which often what the voters want to hear from politicians and policy makers?

Who wants to hear their leaders telling them this is a truly difficult thing which will take for ever to solve (even as the street fires burn and the sirens blare)?

So, in the short-term, neither of these North-Eastern analyses is much better than the 'wicked and sick' North-Western one we discarded early on. While both may well have some substance to them for the longer term , neither seems to offer you any help, as you sit in the hot seat. Of course, they may (or may not) play well to the electorate – just as the North-Western analysis might or might not play well to other parts of the population – but that's just a holding pattern.

The problem is that neither of these two extremes really help to stop the rioting that has already broken out; nor do they help stop the spread of the rioting itself from borough to borough and out beyond the M25 motorway which encircles London.

So can our approach help find a better analysis of what kind of thing the riots are and a better list of what kind of strategy might best address them *here and now*?

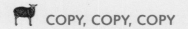

Riots – the long term view

An historical perspective is a great counterbalance to the tyranny of the singular and the myopia that it can bring. History brings a wider context to any given phenomenon: by seeing many instances of the thing in the context of many other things like it, the underlying characteristics often sing out. Without the perspective of history, it's all too easy to misunderstand phenomena.

The first point an historical analysis highlights, is that rioting is more common than we think and that we Brits are particularly good at it. We would like to believe – and we tell the world – that we are a peace-loving people, bounded by a sense of civic order and respect for authority. The reality is rather different and always has been.

In his great historical analysis of rioting and public disorder, written in the shadow of the 1981 Brixton and Toxteth riots, Sociologist Geoffrey Pearson notes:

> 'the myth of "the British way of life" … [is that] … after centuries of domestic peace, the streets of Britain have been suddenly plunged into an unnatural state of disorder that betrays the stable traditions of the past … the real traditions are quite different: that for generations Britain has been plagued by the same fears and problems as today; and that this is something which should require us to reassess the shape of our present difficulties and their prospects for the future.'[68]

Pearson is right. Looking back over history it's clear that riots don't happen all the time in Britain but they do happen

on both a small and a large scale frequently enough for us not to assume any particular instance is an outlier (as politicians and researchers are prone to do).

Rioting highlights in London area 1990-2011

1990 Poll tax riots against introduction of Poll tax, Central

1993 Welling (anti-Nazi) riots, SE London

1995 Brixton riots following death of youth in custody

1996 Rioting in Trafalgar Square area – Euro 1996

1999 Carnival against Capitalism riot, Central

2000 Anti-Capitalist May Day riot, Central

2002 Millwall fans riot outside the New Den, SE London

2009 Upton Park riot: Millwall FC vs. WHUFC, SE London

2010 Student Protests and riots, Central

2011 Anti Cuts protests and riot, Central

2011 London riots proper[69]

Be it riots led by medieval goldsmiths and silk merchants, by hard-pressed West Indian immigrants or by 1960s anti-war protestors; riots shaped by anti-Catholic, anti-Jewish or all-purpose anti-foreigner sentiments; riots led by visiting Australian, American and Canadian servicemen; or riots prompted by unpopular taxes (both Gin, land and Poll-taxes) – rioting and civil disorder runs like a golden thread through British, and particularly London, history.

This is no recent phenomenon: whether the riots are led by by medieval goldsmiths and silk merchants, hard-pressed West Indian immigrants or by 1960s anti-war protestors, fuelled by Anti-Catholic, Anti-Jewish or all-purpose Anti-foreigner sentiments, started by visiting Australian, Canadian or American servicemen or prompted by unpopular taxes on Gin or Land, rioting and civil disorder runs through our history like a golden thread.

Yet we persist in ignoring the record, ignoring that today's occurrences represent a fall from grace, from a better kinder world. Typical of this kind of thing is the 19th-Century philanthropist, Henry Worsley who said:

> 'Any candid judge will acknowledge the manifest superiority of the past century and in an investigation of the causes which have conspired to produce such an unhappy increase of juvenile crime, which is blot upon the age, the altered relations of village life cannot be overlooked.'

It is striking how far we go to distance ourselves from the riotous truth of the British (and London) experience. Why otherwise would we adopt foreign words to describe those who behave this way – the 'hooligan' (Irish) and the 'thug' (from the Hindi)? Conceptualizing rioting this way as alien allows us to put the blame elsewhere and not to see it as part of our world – a natural and not infrequent aspect of our experience, rather than something that is unique and never-before-seen-round-here.

The final learning from a detailed examination of the record of riots and rioting is this: riots come and riots go, howeverso brightly they burn. Rioting is not some once-in-a-lifetime event but a frequent visitor to our streets who then, as quick as a flash, is gone again, leaving the authorities to clear up and find someone to blame. Until the next time.

More news from nowhere

As it happens, our nearest neighbours across the English Channel are also pretty good at civic disorder (and not just Breton Farmers blockading British lamb imports). In fact 2005 was a French bumper year with the 'burning of the banlieues' (suburbs) a notable incendiary success. The largely immigrant population of the impoverished towns that circle 'the French capital responded to many years of racial prejudice, inequality, economic struggle and so on with a long-lasting outburst of arson, fighting the police and old-fashioned rioting'.

Not to be outdone, the Australian city of Sydney was also engulfed by the Beach Riots in the sun- and alcohol-drenched run-up to the Australian Christmas holidays – for more than a week, running battles between local youths and the neighbours they called 'lebs' (young men of eastern Mediterranean origin) swept through the western suburbs and beyond.

And of course, we have the examples of various disorder incidents in the US, not least the excellently documented 1957 Detroit riots.

The point being that the 2011 London riots were far from an isolated instance – we and our neighbours are jolly good at civil disorder. And that's a good thing, in that it provides us with a huge dataset to ask 'what kind of thing' questions.

What's a riot?

So what can we learn about the phenomenon from these different instances of rioting?

UCL professor Matthew Moran underlines in *Le Monde Diplomatique* (January 2012) that looking across time and space enables us to see similarities in the phenomena:

> *'the riot as a process exhibits features that often remain constant in different contexts (the events that trigger the violence, response to the violence, media coverage, etc.). So comparisons between different episodes of rioting are valuable.'*

Recipe for a riot

Whatever the immediate spark, rioting tends to require a number of preconditions to start:

1. A large number of young men available for rioting (un- or underemployed) with nothing to do.
2. High levels of disaffection among this group with the authorities and strong feelings of injustice (for whatever reason).
3. Good weather (this is often an underappreciated factor but rain and rioting don't sit well together).

In the case of the 2011 UK riots, all three of these were present: while nearly half of the rioters were in some form of education, the majority of the other half were unemployed unskilled young men – a demographic which has suffered particularly badly from the fallout of the global financial crisis.

As the *Financial Times* analysis observed:

'when London's neighbourhoods are clustered into 10 groups on the basis of their average income, there are 11 additional riot suspects for every step down in the deprivation ranking.'[70]

And they were more available than they might otherwise have been because their youth clubs, projects and centres had been closed as a result of local government cuts. As a result these young men (and women) were living much of their life on the street with each other and thus frequently interacting with authorities such as the police – often in a way that leaves resentments and fears burning year after year. As the excellent *The Guardian*/LSE study observed:

'Where young law-abiding people are repeatedly targeted there is a very real danger that stop and search will have a corrosive effect on their relationship with the police.'[71]

Of those interviewed, 73% claimed that they had been stopped and searched in the previous 12 months. This is eight times more likely than the incidence of the rest of the population in London. Similar figures are reported in the post-analyses of the 2005 Paris riots.

"All the ingredients for riots were ready and available in August 2011."

To top it all, the summer of 2011 had been a relatively good one so these young people were out on the streets more often than they might otherwise have been.

This much the UK authorities should have known, really.

Complex, complex

Riots may be seen to have many causes – depending at what level you choose to examine them: individuals may be seen to be wicked or sick agents, acting independently from each other or the objects of big socio-economic forces from which there is no escape. And individuals report the experience and the mechanics of their involvement differently and in a way which may or may not reflect the reality of things.

But the way riots suddenly break out and spread suggests that they are *complex* phenomena – mostly self-organizing and unpredictable.

You *can* have the conditions but no spark or the wrong kind of spark and nothing will happen. This is why riots seem to blindside us so often.

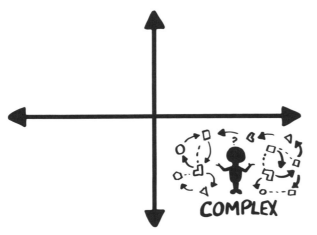

COMPLEX

It would seem that rioting is shaped by fundamentally social factors (so rioting is on the Eastern end of our map) and fluid ones at that (South-Eastern rather than Northern): it is rare that 'organizers' or 'leaders' take control of rioters – more often than not the outbreaks of this kind of behaviour are spontaneous and they spread by people doing what those around them are doing, often just copying or looking to outdo each other.

The 'influential' hypothesis is a very popular analysis in lots of circumstances – in marketing as much as in public order challenges. We'd all feel a lot more comfortable if we could pin any phenomenon on the actions of a few (wicked/biddable/knowledgeable) individuals. Not least because we can then target those 'hubs' in the social network which they supposedly dominate. Unfortunately this is not the way most social networks structure themselves in the modern world (on- or offline).[72]

In fact the early suggestion, by both London politicians and the media, that gangs were driving the rioting was disproved by later analysis (just as had been the case in Paris some years previously). Indeed, it turned out that a number of street gangs agreed a four-day truce in their ongoing mutual hostilities to enable all their members to embrace the riots fully without the distraction of gang rivalry.

As one participant told the *Financial Times*, 'People just got involved for free stuff. They took what they could. Someone else started it so they just jumped in, because this is a poor area. Someone basically opened the door and people just walked in.'[73]

The Metropolitan Police Service report acknowledges as much, noting 'either the violence was spontaneous without any degree of forethought or...a level of tension existed among sections of the community that was not identified through the [Met's extensive] community engagement.' Or both, maybe.

Fuel to the flames

Moreover the media's over-enthusiastic depiction of graphic imagery and its dystopian discourse can and did serve merely to amplify the sense of how popular the violence was. The US media have learned over the years that too high profile coverage of the kind of high-school gun massacres that bedevil those institutions can and does encourage repetition elsewhere.[74]

It happens again and again – just as with copycat suicides which were discussed in *HERD* – Monkey See, Monkey Do shapes the spread of these kinds of incidents. Particularly when displayed on a big shiny 42' TV screen in HD colour. From Virginia Tech in 2007 to the University of California at Santa Barbara in 2014, lone disaffected individuals find themselves modelling the glorified pseudo-heroic model of the outsider gunman they've seen on TV to shape their own actions.

If mainstream media had a central (unintentional) role in the spread of the London riots, social media proved rather less important – unlike the post-match analysis of the Sydney riots which revealed the importance of peer-to-peer messaging (SMS especially) in helping rioters co-ordinate their efforts – during London riots social media seemed to have been rather less important in the successful spread of the behaviour than the mainstream media initially claimed.

It did, however, lead to some unintentional comedy. One (famously incompetent) would-be rioter in the West Midlands felt emboldened by the mainstream media coverage to create a (public) event page on Facebook for the 'Mob Hill Massive Northwich Lootin'.

'Smash d[o]wn in Northwich Town', he wrote, encouraging fellow rioters to meet on 9 August, between 13:00 and 16:00 BST, 'behind maccies' (the McDonald's restaurant in Northwich town centre).

Both he and his gormless sidekick who commented on the page 'We'll need to get this kickin off all over' experienced a rest at Her Majesty's Pleasure.

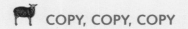

The violence virus

This would make a lot of sense to Gary Slutkin, an American epidemiologist by training, who spent the early part of his career working in Africa trying to counter the spread of infectious diseases like TB, cholera and HIV/Aids. Key to his success in tackling these kinds of life or death struggles was developing interventions appropriate to the behaviour of those involved, without moralizing over their ethics, motivations or character – the 'kinda' strategy for the 'kinda' behaviour, even.

A lot of the time this meant digging down into the reality of the real lives of those involved in the transmission of a particular disease, using outreach workers much like those targeted, in order to find and encourage alternatives to the default choices.

❝ The main challenge is to stop seeing all violent people as bad. ❞

On his return to the US in 1995, Slutkin found himself thinking hard about what the US media was calling an 'epidemic' of violence sweeping across so many great American cities. He wondered if his epidemiological models and strategies might work as well for a metaphorical 'epidemic' as for a medical one.

He saw the spread of violence as a social phenomenon not the result of individual pathologies. The data from other fields point strongly in this direction. *Social* is how violence gets transmitted: from the 30% of child abuse victims who become abusers to the 100% increase in your likelihood to commit violent gun crime if you are exposed to an incident of it.[75]

> '*The main challenge in the United States is overcoming the idea that those who commit violence are "bad" people and that the way to respond to violence is with punishment.*'[76]

Go back earlier in this challenge to the Prime Minister's description of 'wicked' and 'evil' individuals responsible for the London riots. Ask yourself, does this really reflect how you now think this kind of behaviour is spread and adopted?

❝ Getting between people (not between their ears). ❞

Sound familiar?

So how does Slutkin's approach tackle things?

Most of us have been in late night situations in which an ugly atmosphere can suddenly turn from bad to worse – in which violence emerges in response to some imagined sleight or insult; in which violence is the go-to resolution, violence the gag-response. If threatened or challenged by competitors or strangers, groups of young men can rapidly – under the right or wrong – shift modes from peaceful co-existence to violence. This is viral.

Just as with his health interventions, Slutkin's anti-violence work uses 'interrupters' – incredibly brave and skilled individuals – who, like the Forest Service's fire-jumpers, leap into the searing heart of a human situation to stop it spreading. Encouraging those prompted to escalate to violence by, for example, a perceived slight to their group identity or some personal 'disrespect' not to go where the norms of the culture in which they lived or the behaviour of their heroes and their icons point.

And the results are pretty striking: the state-wide New York programme intervened in more than 400 incidents in 2011 and in the first half of that year more than 200 separate incidents – many of which would have otherwise led to violent behaviour and large scale disorder – were defused by his team.[77]

Slutkin's award-winning programme 'CeaseFire' now works in a number of US cities – including Chicago and Baltimore – but most importantly for our purposes, it works in the space *between people* not on them.

'If we can really understand that people become violent through a contagious process and that the people who are violent have a health issue, then the disease control approach makes even more sense.'

The point being that to stop the spread of something, you really need to think about transmission and get between infectious agent and potential victim. In the space between people, not the space between their ears.

If violence spreads socially, you need to step in to stop the spread.

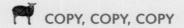

What would you do to stop the spread of the rioting?

Why not have a quick review of the South-East strategies again and see which strike you as most useful to pursue in your attempts to stop the riot from spreading. Which three things will you try first?

Here are my suggestions:

> **Suggested Short-term Strategies**
>
> Help people see each others' enthusiasm
>
> Make punishment more visible
>
> Give them things to do (or watch together)

1. Help people (not to) see each other's enthusiasm

It is imperative to follow this strategy *but in reverse*: to stop individual rioters and prospective recruits to the riots being able to see what others are doing.

During the 2011 riots, there was a lot of noise made in the media about rioters' use of the new-fangled social media platforms to communicate with each other and co-ordinate their attacks.

However, if the authorities had worked with the platforms to listen and follow the conversations online, they might have had more forewarning of an impending outbreak of violence and thus been able to respond more quickly and precisely.

Perhaps a more determined hunt for those using social media to celebrate or co-ordinate violence would also have helped provide intelligence rather than merely deter the use of it in this way. This was part of the response of the authorities to the Sydney Beach riots of 2005: a communications-led lock down.

A rather less directly effective (but perhaps more symbolic) course of action would be to simply shut down the services entirely. Though this might also unintentionally confirm some of the fears of the population at large – as a power-outage would do.

2. Make punishment more visible and thus seem more likely

One of the issues for individuals who found themselves involved in the rioting, often commented in subsequent interviews, is this: the apparently low chance of being caught – police were caught napping and often had to retreat leaving the streets to the rioters. While the instinct of many commentators for retributive justice was understandable perhaps the real issue was how quickly and early to publicize the likelihood of being caught and the significant punishment which would follow.

Part of this was addressed by drafting in police reinforcements from across the UK and having them display themselves publically. As the Prime Minister admitted, 'there were simply far too few police deployed onto our streets'. Similarly, the Metropolitan Police Service's later report agreed that 'there were not enough officers to deal with unprecedented scale and geographical spread of the disorder'. However, it was also important to ensure that those caught were quickly processed through the legal system and their punishment made public and visible.

As CPS chief, Keir Starmer wisely commented (c/o *The Guardian*[78]):

> ' They [rioters] gamble on: "Am I going to get caught?" ... And if the answer is: "I'm now watching on the television some other people who had been caught 24 hours or 48 hours after they were on the streets with us" – I think that's a very powerful message.'

3. Give people things to do (or watch) together

In the long run, it would be helpful to find things for the young men at the heart of these riots to do which didn't bring them into daily contact with the law enforcement authorities and the opportunity to riot. Equally, more time in the workplace would also help (but in fact many of those convicted in the summer of 2011 were in low-paid or part-time work).

It's not that I'm suggesting the short-term riot in progress can be solved by these things, but if you want to make rioting less likely in the future then reducing the availability of the key demographic is a big priority.

Of course, if we've learned anything from understanding the historical record, it is that these things pass – complex phenomena come and go and riots almost always tend to fade away. Undoubtedly this would be a very unpopular strategy to suggest to a politician – they like to be seen as action heroes, doing things to save us from the bad guys.

The bottom line is this: even something as scary and distant from the cosy world of marketing and civic society as riots is easy to get to grips with if only you ask yourself what kind of thing you're dealing with before you jump to strategy and tactics.

This chapter has been about putting the questions and the tools to work which the rest of the book has explored.

It has been about 'praxis' rather than 'theorie': doing rather than mere thinking.

The point being not that you have the definitive answer to any of the 4 challenges I have set you.

Not least because there aren't any 'definitive' answers – in how to launch a new product or change a behaviour or deal with civic emergencies (let's hope none of us actually find ourselves responsible for the latter …).

Rather, the point of this chapter is to give you a chance to work this way: to give you hands-on experience in strategizing using our big 3 questions, the map, the strategy archive and the other tools and tricks discussed above. In working in this copycat way.

The basic themes here are the same as we've discussed throughout:

Focus on the behaviour and the choice style of that behaviour. What it is and not what you've been told.

Beware the Singularity: ask yourself what kind of thing this is?

Identify strategies from elsewhere that have been successful in changing that kind of behavioural challenge.

And steal them by copying – turn them into things that you can test in the real world.

This chapter is about you and your experiences, so the conclusions are yours:

- What have you learned from these exercises?
- In what ways does this approach help you do strategy?
- In what ways do you feel uncomfortable?
- In what ways did it make things easier/better?
- What kinds of things should we tell other people?

Take a moment to note down your thoughts.

And if you feel like it, please share them with us at **CopyCopyCopy.co.**

CONCLUSION

AFTERWORD

> Do what I do. Hold tight and pretend it's a plan.
> —*Doctor Who*, Season 7, BBC Wales

SAVING MORE LIVES WITH F1

There are few fields of human activity in which the advances of modern science and technology deliver such striking rewards as surgery, particularly cardiac surgery.

As Martin Elliott, Gresham Professor of Physic, UCL Professor of Paediatric Cardiothoracic Surgery and Co-Medical Director of The Great Ormond Street Hospital for Sick Children points out, within just one professional lifetime, mortality rates in his field have gone from virtually 100% to single figures. That is, from almost everybody dying on or after the operating table to one in which almost nobody does – just since he has been working. Thanks to innovative practices and the application of new technologies.

Even in Martin's speciality, *paediatric* heart surgery, things have improved to such a degree that operating successfully on a 2 week old baby with a congenital heart defect – a 'hole in the heart', say – is no longer the stuff of newspaper headlines, as it was a decade or two ago. It remains, however, an incredibly difficult and challenging thing to do for a living and something about which its practitioners are rightly proud.

And yet, Martin and his colleagues at Great Ormond Street Hospital continue to strive for new ways to improve their performance.

One part of this mission involves the development of a common means of comparing outcomes – curiously, there is no accepted international standard measurement for surgical performance. This is an essential first step in helping his profession identify and learn from best practice in its own field (copying nearby experts if you like).

But the other part of the mission is about learning from people and practices outside their field: from the noisy expensive world of Formula 1 racing.

Go round again[79]

Back in 2003, after an intensive and exhausting day in theatre, Martin and his colleague Allan Goldman (head of the paediatric ITU team at Great Ormond Street) found themselves trying to unwind by watching an F1 race on TV. Surgery is exhausting and the long and very precise procedures that GOSH is famous for are particularly so. At the end of them, some staff head to the pub, others to the gym, others simply slump in front of the TV.

As is so often the case, a tired mind can sometimes see things that others don't. In this case two tired minds saw the same curious things: first, the striking similarity between the geography of the operating theatre – it's layout and the nature of the multiple skillsets ranged around the bed – and that of the large pit stop team working on a car that had come in for a pitstop.

And – more strikingly, perhaps – the difference in the speed and precision of the two teams at a turnover: the medical team seemed positively sluggish by comparison with the pit-stop team, especially at handover.

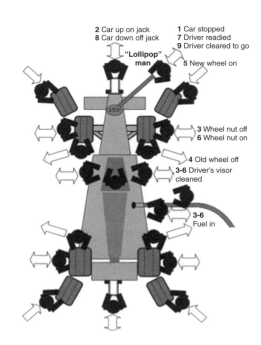

ON THE RIGHT TRACK

Intrigued, Elliott and Goldman invited the Newbury-based McLaren F1 team to tell them about pit stop manoeuvres and how to get good at them. A great deal of emphasis, they learned, was placed on human factor analysis and in particular on eradicating small errors rather than large ones. Small errors are the enemy, as they slip by in the heat of the race.

So much – it turns out – the team at GOSH were clear about already. A colleague, Professor Marc De Leval, had previously published a controversial study of just this kind of human factor analysis of the transitions from surgery to ITU which concluded that adding up these small human mistakes created a strong correlation with bad outcomes for patients.

Think of it this way: a patient coming out of the operating theatre is plugged into any number of machines, wires pumps and feeds – it's like a spaghetti tangle around a tiny prone, vulnerable patient. The slightest error in reconnecting these can have disastrous consequences. The theatre staff are just plain exhausted, after several hours in prep and several intense more doing some of the toughest work in medical surgery on the smallest and most vulnerable patients. And the fresh ITU team just want the

handoff – want the precious bundle in their care, without interference. It's a recipe for small but life-threatening errors creeping in.

FORZA ITALIA

Elliott and Goldman weren't satisfied by the conceptual insight: they wanted to know precisely how F1 pit teams get so good – what practices they could steal. So - now with the addition of human factor expert, Ken Catchpole – they travelled to Ferrari's HQ in Italy to meet with Nigel Stepney, Ferrari's Technical Director. One of the first things they did was play him video footage of their medical handovers and describe the process in pictures.

Stepney was horrified. Whereas an F1 team is prepared for any number of different situations, drilled and choreographed to perfection, the medical teams respond to what happens in the moment; whereas the 'lollipop man' ushers the driver in and gives the signal to go, nobody is necessarily in charge of the handover from surgical to ITU team. Each F1 team member is trained and trained to avoid minor errors, but the surgical team are trained to avoid the big stuff (in whatever way seems most appropriate at the time). Indeed, many have their own idiosyncratic and successful practices, based on training and experience. F1 teams have a single checklist to make sure that all the small things get done right. In many surgical handover teams, there is no checklist: these highly trained professionals just get on and make things happen.

Going through this exercise, testing and the institutionalizing in the hospital some of the best practice in F1 has enabled the team at GOSH to improve outcomes by a significant margin. Just by the simple measure of error counts, Martin's team has reduced these by 40%+. With significant impact on patient outcomes. Fewer errors in this small moment – the handover from surgical team to ITU – mean better results for patients. And that's what really matters, not where the practices that prevent them come from.

And now, nearly a decade on, other surgical teams in other hospitals – both in the UK and the US – now readily use these simple practices to improve patient care.

COPY COPY COPY

This story is not really about Martin or his team or surgery or indeed, about F1. Instead, it captures some of the essential ideas I've tried to convey in this book.

The central role of copying in creating value, solving problems and driving innovation.

The importance of loose (in this case by copying from afar), rather than tight copying.

The need to ask what kind of thing ('kinda') questions: in this case, it was crucial to see that the similarity between the patient on the operating table and the F1 driver at the pit stop and the teams' arrangement around them. Without this appreciating that they were both similar kinds of things, the transfer of ideas and practices from one context to the other would just have been guesswork.

The need to 'show me what you mean': turning things from one place into things in another, rather than just leaving it at a conceptual level of similarity. And, finally, the need to test and learn.

Of course, it will be really great if and when Martin and his colleagues and collaborators around the world crack the problem of a universally accepted way of measuring patient outcomes so that good and bad practice can be shared and among those in the field, but while they struggle with that, this simple approach of learning from another – quite distant – field seems to be capable of bringing great (perhaps greater value) and doing so, far more quickly.

IF THIS, THEN WHEN ...?

I wrote *HERD* to try to get folk who do strategy to see the people whose behaviour they sought to change as they really are – I wanted to draw a better map, for their many different journeys, if you like.

However, I deliberately held back from giving the reader too many specific (or cheap and easy, as I then felt) answers. I really wanted people to use the new map the book described (and the subsequent *I'll Have What She's Having*) as fuel for their own rethinking of what to do.

" Get good at copying and using other people's work. "

As it happens, since *HERD* came out, I've enjoyed any number of conversations with people in different disciplines – in marketing and the military, in government and brandland, in the UK, the US and all around the world. The one thing I always find myself doing is trying to work out specific answers to the new world view that *HERD* argued for.

I've been lucky enough to collaborate with partners and clients who want to experiment and achieve new things, so we've been able to develop lots of new things – new research tools, new analytics techniques, new ways to engage audiences, new job titles (most of which we copied from somewhere else, naturally).

WHAT DO WE DO THEN?

So now I think there's a need for a more direct answer to the question, 'what do we do different then, if the world is like you say it is?'

This what this book has been about: trying to articulate how we should change the way we do strategy.

And the answer is this: get good at copying and using the works of others in your strategizing; abandon at the same time all the hangover of 'originality', of 'creative genius' or 'innovation-as-invention' as I described in Chapter 2.

If the landscape for which we are strategizing – in terms of competition and consumer behaviour alike – were as mechanical and 'Newtonian' as we all used to think it was then the old reductionist ways of doing strategy would be fine: seeing every problem as a singular one and the job of the strategist as being to examine its initial conditions (digging deep into the detail) so that a unique and logical solution would reveal itself (while all false answers would be thrown away).

- You *could* take your time doing the things that made reductionist perfection.
- You *could* spend as much resource as you wanted, creating an army of strategists to get the strategy 100% right before you started to implement anything.
- You *could* pursue ready-aim-fire with confidence in a disciplined and grown-up manner.

But – as I and many others like me have argued – this is NOT how the world is. The landscape in which marketers, policy makers and managers operate is complex, shifting and unpredictable.

Some things stay the same for a very long time and then suddenly shift; some are in constant rapid flux; some even seem to be in two states at the same time – unchanging and changing.

" You have to try multiple things and learn how the world responds to them – rinse and repeat, rapido. "

You can't in this kind of landscape presume on the old model of strategizing: of moving step-by-considered-step towards 'the' answer (singular). You have to try multiple things and learn how the world responds to them – rinse and repeat, rapido.

And you can't hope to have all these ideas yourself – however smart you are. You're going to need to use the ultimate human advantage (no, not cake, although that is in my view rarely wrong).

You're going to need to learn to use the brains of those around you better:

- To copy better (by which you will remember I mean *worse*).
- To copy more loosely, to copy from further away.

This is the only way you can possibly hope to have enough ideas, fast enough to keep up.

" Copying well/badly is the strategist's answer to 'what do I differently?' "

Copying well/badly is a priority skill for the strategist who's dealing with people problems.

Copying well/badly is an easy way to live in the modern world of business and organizations.

WHAT NEXT?

As I've been developing this line of thinking, here are some of the challenges people have made and some of the answers I've given them. It might help further clarify what I'm proposing.

Aren't you just making us do strategy by numbers?

No quite the opposite: this is strategy by humans (humans being the best at copying). Making sure that you copy success, but loosely and from a distance. And that you copy multiple things rather than just imagine one thing is going to suffice.

Aren't you de-skilling the guild by giving all the answers away?

Not at all: that is to misunderstand how this approach to strategy works. You still have to understand the targeted behaviour and the mechanics which shaped it but as a member of a class of behaviours rather than a unique one-off that requires a similarly unique answer. This makes strategy more useful rather than what one old art director famously called, 'some sweeping generalizations and pointless number crunching'. And in any case, making the pattern books of architecture available to pro- and amateur builders alike didn't exactly destroy the architectural profession, did it?

Isn't this just formalizing what good strategists do?

There may be more of a hint of truth to this challenge. Many of us have something like a mental strategy 'pattern book' that we use in our work, it's just that few of us catalogue them explicitly.

The difference here is:

1. The strategies are sorted according to their success in addressing different kinds of choice.
2. The sheer number of them makes it harder to default to 'my favourite club'.

In other words, the sheer number of them help you copy more loosely (a good thing) and copy from far away.

Are these all the strategies there are?

No: the book contains 52 different types of successful strategy that my collaborators and I have observed working elsewhere. I may well introduce novelty into them over time – in later editions, perhaps – to stop them going stale.

I hope it's a comprehensive list but in no way does it claim to be exhaustive. You may want to add your own, too. If you have any suggestions, please send them to CopyCopyCopy.co. The best will be included and you'll be credited.

What if my category isn't reflected in the examples in the book?

Don't worry, the point is – as suggested in Chapter 2 – to make you learn from outside the category. In fact, if you find your category represented in a particular example, then I'd find another example instead. We don't want any single white female strategizing here, do we?

Does this strategy pattern book replace the need for testing and evaluation?

No, not at all. This is all about creating things to test and testing them earlier by making them into prototypes – doing more testing, rather than less testing, but doing it earlier. However, given that the contents of the pattern books are all successful strategies in other contexts and the way they've been sorted by their ability to impact on different kinds of choice, they should – *should* – provide you with more confidence going into tests (and less of the anxiety that the single-solution test gives all of us forced to work that way).

Is this a replacement for the whole 'agile' process obsession in business today? Or, something else?

Put simply, it's the fuel for agile processes: it gives you the content that can drive agile processes more effectively. And if you're not formally 'agile', then it can help you be so more easily.

ORIGINALITY AND COPYING REDUX

At the start of this book, and woven all the way through it, are some examples of great innovators – great originals who made amazing and remarkable things but revealed that for all their 'singularity', they too copied the work of others; indeed, they rely on the work of others to do their own innovation.

From scientists like Isaac Newton to sports coaches like Steve Brailsford, great artists of the past like Picasso and Shakespeare to modern storytellers like Philip Pullman and George RR Martin: all of these walked the same path of copying (even though some found it harder to admit to). All of them we acknowledge innovators and producers of extraordinary originality in their work, yet each and every one achieved the status of 'genius' by being a magpie: a borrower and stealer of other peoples work.

None more so than the late great Elvis Presley – 'an original in the age of copycats' and yet copycat par-excellence. Elvis dreamed all his life of being extraordinary and emulating his childhood hero, Captain Marvel Jr (which probably explains some of his crazier stunts later on, such as his offer to then President Nixon of leading the war on drugs armed with his ju-jitsu tricks and his own narcotics dependency). Elvis never found it easy living up to the idea of Elvis, reliant as he was on the audience to confirm him in that role. Few do – it can often make things harder – one of my old colleagues

(no Elvis, he) felt so stressed by the need to be a 'genius' he paid tens of thousands of dollars every year to keep a certain trends report under lock and key so that he could pass its findings off as his own and thus maintain his 'guru' status.

So maybe one of the most useful things the approach in this book can encourage is for you to give up the idea of your own singularity – the special status that comes from being a genius at solving tough problems. Maybe it's time for the innovator and the strategist to step back out of the limelight and accept that what we do best, we do on the shoulders of others, using the work of others far away and often unnamed: we do best what we do by copying well (or badly).

Let's put an end to this exceptionalism and perhaps start to be just a little more 'menschlich' – more human and happy to be of the common sort. Remember this: originality arises in the space between you and other people, not primarily in the space between your own ears. And in using it as you do to make new and different things, you are only doing what makes all of us human.

> *'Prince, Subject, Father, Son, are things forgot, For every man alone thinks he hath got To be a Phoenix, and that then can be None of that kind, of which he is, but he.'*
> John Donne, *An Anatomy of the World*

You never know. You might enjoy being human.

REFERENCES

1 http://rsnr.royalsocietypublishing.org/content/62/3/289.full.

2 RA Bentley (2008) Random drift versus selection in academic vocabulary. PLoS ONE 3(8): e3057. doi: 10.1371/journal.pone.0003057.

3 http://www.cyclesportmag.com/features/inside-the-mind-of-dave-brailsford/.

4 http://www.bbc.co.uk/sport/0/olympics/19174302.

5 Interview BBC Radio 4 Saturday Live, 7 September 2013.

6 Mikal Gilmore (2014) 'George R.R. Martin: The Rolling Stone Interview', *Rolling Stone Magazine*, 23.4.14 online at http://www.rollingstone.com/movies/news/george-r-r-martin-the-rolling-stone-interview-20140423#ixzz33m5vlfSS.

7 O Jones (2015) Every Great Individual stands on the shoulders of others, *Guardian Online*, Sunday 4th January 2015.

8 Karl Marx (1845) *Theses on Feuerbach in Marx/Engels Selected Works*, Vol 1. pp. 13–15.

9 BBC News online: http://www.bbc.co.uk/news/uk-wales-south-east-wales-19765768.

10 http://www.youtube.com/watch?v=ZsKFTFBMst8.

11 Online at http://www.elvis-history-blog.com/elvis-milton-berle.html.

12 http://en.wikipedia.org/wiki/Elvis_Presley

13 http://www.dailymail.co.uk/news/article-2233797/Bernard-Lansky-death-Legendary-clothier-dressed-Elvis-Presley-dies-aged-85.html.

14 John Arlidge (2014) 'iPraise indeed for Stever "Stinger" Jobs', *Sunday Times* online.

15 http://www.poynter.org/latest-news/everyday-ethics/177809/whats-wrong-with-jonah-lehrer-plagiarizing-himself/.

16 Chief amongst Biden's accusers was the same Maureen Dowd who has herself been challenged about plagiarism more recently.

17 'Joe Biden Plagiarised Kinnock Speech', *Telegraph*, 23 August 2008. See also David Greenberg (2008) 'The Write Stuff: Why Biden's plagiarism shouldn't be forgotten', *Slate Magazine* online at http://www.slate.com/articles/news_and_politics/history_lesson/2008/08/the_write_stuff.html.

18 Policy statement, 1944, of the Youth League of the African National Congress.

19 Ibid.

20 D Tutu (2000) *No Future without Forgiveness: A Personal Overview of South Africa's Truth and Reconciliation Commission*, London: Rider & Co.

21 AN Meltzoff and MK Moore (1977). 'Imitation of Facial and Manual Gestures by Human Neonates', *Science*, 198, 75–78; AN Meltzoff (1999) 'Born to Learn: What Infants Learn from Watching Us', in N Fox and JG Worhol (eds.), *The Role of Early Experience in Infant Development*, Skillman, NJ: Pediatric Institute Publications.

22 This is much tougher for the offspring of other apes – we are unique amongst them in 'alloparenting' (sharing parenting with those other than the genetic parents) as Sarah Blaffer Hrdy points out in her 2011 book *Mothers and Others: the Evolutionary Origins of Mutual Understanding*, Cambridge, MA: Harvard University Press.

23 RA Bentley, MB Earls and M Obrien (2011) I'll Have What She's Having – Mapping Social Behaviour Cambridge, MA: MIT Press.

24 D Kahneman (2012) Thinking Fast, Thinking Slow, London: Penguin.

25 L Rendell, R Boyd, D Cownden, M Enquist, K Eriksson, MW Feldman, L Fogarty, S Ghirlanda, T Lillicrap, and KN Laland, 'Why Copy Others? Insights from the Social Learning Strategies Tournament', Science, 9 April, 328(5975): 208–13. doi: 10.1126/science.1184719. Online at http://www.ncbi.nlm.nih.gov/pubmed/20378813.

26 *MovieMaker Magazine #53*, Winter, 22 January 2004.

27 Title of the 2nd studio album by Talking Heads (1978).

28 Online at http://birdabroad.wordpress.com/2011/07/20/are-you-listening-steve-jobs/.

29 PM Nattermann (2000) Best Practice does not equal Best Strategy, *McKinsey Quarterly*, 2.

30 J Schumpeter (1911) *Theorie der wirtschaftlichen Entwicklung* translated as (1934) *The Theory of Economic Development: An inquiry into profits, capital, credit, interest and the business cycle*.

31 M Gilmore (2014) *Rolling Stone Magazine* (see the Introduction).

32 http://magicalnihilism.com/2009/11/07/get-excited-and-make-things/.

33 Film, music, script and narration by Temujin Doran. http://www.studiocanoe.com/index.php?...http://www.directorsnotes.com/2012/03/06/the-story-of-keep-calm-and-carry-on/.

34 R Sennett (2008) *The Craftsman*, New Haven, CT: Yale University Press.

35 C Darwin (1859) *On the Origin of Species by Means of Natural Selection, or the Preservation of Favoured Races in the Struggle for Life*, London: Murray.

36 http://www.bbc.co.uk/history/historic_figures/watt_james.shtml.

37 C Leadbeater (2009) *We-Think: Mass Innovation, Mass Production*, London: Profile Books.

38 The significance of this will become clear shortly.

39 *Father Ted*, Series 2, Episode 2, 'Hell'.

40 Fansite: http://www.isihac.co.uk/games/ostttoae/ostttoae-d.html.

41 TS Eliot (1921) *The Sacred Wood*, New York: Alfred A. Knopf.

42 A Damasio (2006) *Descartes' Error: Emotion, Reason and the Human Brain*, London: Vintage.

43 Robert Louis Stephenson, Essay 193 cited in *Paperwork: Fiction and Mass Mediacy in the Paper Age* by Kevin Mclaughlin.

44 From the Latin – 'I draw therefore I am'.

45 Steven Pinker (2005) 'College Makeover', *Slate Magazine*, 16 November 2005, http://www.slate.com/articles/news_and_politics/college_week/2005/11/college_makeover.html.

46 R Sennett (2008) *The Craftsman*, New Haven, CT: Yale University Press.

47 Austin Kleon (2012) *Steal Like an Artist – 10 Things Nobody Ever Told you about Being Creative*, New York: Workman Press.

48 http://austinkleon.com/2011/06/11/interviews/.

49 John Snow, letter to the editor *Medical Times* and *Gazette* 9: 321–22, 23 September 1854.

50 See Earls (2007) *HERD – How to Change Mass Behavior by Harnessing Our True Nature*, Chichester: John Wiley & Sons; RA Bentley, M Earls and MJ O'Brien (2011) *I'll Have What She's Having – Mapping Social Behavior*, Cambridge, MA: MIT Press.

51 http://www.youtube.com/watch?v=rMMHUzm22oE.

52 Bentley, Earls and O'Brien (2011) *I'll Have What She's Having*. See also RA Bentley, MJ O'Brien and W Brock 'Mapping Collective Behavior in the Big-data Era', *Behavioral and Brain Sciences* 37: 63–119.

53 Matthew J Salganik, Peter Sheridan Dodds and Duncan J Watts (2006) 'Experimental Study of Inequality and Unpredictability in an Artificial Cultural Market', *Science*, 10 February 2006: 311(5762): 854–56; Matthew J Salganik and Duncan J Watts (2008) 'Leading the Herd Astray: An Experimental Study of Self-Fulfilling Prophecies in an Artificial Cultural Market', *Social Psychology Quarterly*, 2008 Fall: 74(4): 338.

54 Latin – roughly translated as 'disinclined to reveal secrets'.

55 http://www.washingtonpost.com/wp-dyn/content/article/2006/02/24/AR2006022400823.html.

56 See Earls (2003) *Welcome to the Creative Age*, Chichester: John Wiley & Sons, Earls (2007) *HERD* and my discussion with UeberBlogger Hugh Macleod at http://gapingvoid.com/2008/10/18/the-purpose-idea-ten-questions-for-mark-earls/ for more details on purpose ideas.

57 N Taleb (2013) *Anti-fragile: Things that Gain from Disorder*, London: Penguin.

58 Kim Erwin (2013) *Communication the New: Methods to Shape and Accelerate Innovation*, Chichester: John Wiley & Sons.

59 Cited in Erwin (2013).

60 Ed Catmull (2014) *Creativity Inc. Overcoming the Unseen Forces that Stand in the Way of True Inspiration*, London/New York: Bantam Press.

REFERENCES

61 Catmull (2014).

62 Mid-term review.

63 Herminia Ibarra (2015) By Being Authentic, You May Just Be Conforming, *HBR Online*, Jan 19, 2015.

64 Jonathan Sachs, 'Reversing the Decay of London Undone', *Wall Street Journal,* 20 August 2011, http://online.wsj.com/news/articles/SB10001424053111903639404576516252066723110.

65 *Daily Mail*, 9 August 2011.

66 Agatha Christie (1933) *The Thirteen Problems*, Ch. 6.

67 Rebecca Joy Novell, 'The summer's riots happened because we didn't listen to young people', *The Guardian*, 18 November 2011, http://www.theguardian.com/social-care-network/social-life-blog/2011/nov/18/riots-happened-listen-young-people.

68 G Pearson (1983) *Hooligan: A History of Respectable Fears*, Basingstoke: Palgrave Macmillan.

69 Sourced from http://en.wikipedia.org/wiki/List_of_riots_in_London.

70 S Gainsbury and N Culzac, 'Rioting Link to Deprivation Revealed', http://www.ft.com, 4 September 2011.

71 P Lewis, T Newburn, M Taylor and J Ball, 'Rioters Say Anger with Police Fuelled Summer Unrest', 5 December 2011, http://www.theguardian.com/uk/2011/dec/05/anger-police-fuelled-riots-study.

72 SP Borgotti, A Mehra, DJ Brass and G Labianca (2009) 'Network Analysis in the Social Sciences', *Science* 13 February 2009, 323(5916), 892–95, DOI: 10.1126/science.1165821.

73 Sally Gainsbury and Natasha Culzac (2011) 'Rioting Link to Deprivation Revealed', *Financial Times*, 4 September 2011.

74 Nigel Barber (2012) 'The Human Beast' (online, *Psychology Today*) http://www.psychologytoday.com/blog/the-human-beast/201207/copycat-killings.

75 http://www.wired.co.uk/magazine/archive/2013/06/ideas-bank/like-many-other-diseases-violence-can-be-cured.

76 http://www.ssireview.org/blog/entry/interrupting_the_transmission_of_violence.

77 http://www.theguardian.com/uk/2011/aug/14/rioting-disease-spread-from-person-to-person.

78 F Bawdon, P Lewis and T Newburn, 'Rapid riot prosecutions more important than long sentences, says Keir Starmer', 3 July 2012, http://www.theguardian.com/uk/2012/jul/03/riot-prosecutions-sentences-keir-starmer.

79 N Gautam (2006) Hospital races to learn lessons of Ferrari crew, *Wall Street Journal* (online) & KR Catchpole, MR de Leval, A McEwan, N Pigott, MJ Elliot, A McQuillan, C MacDonald and AJ Goldman (2007) Patient handover from surgery to intensive care: using Formula 1 pit-stop and aviation models to improve safety and quality, *Pediatric Anesthesia* 17, 470-478.

ABOUT THE AUTHOR

Author photo supplied by Emli Bendixen

Mark Earls is an award-winning writer, speaker and strategist whose work to champion the application of contemporary behavioural and cognitive science to the practice of marketing and behaviour change has had a significant effect on how those disciplines understand human behaviour. In particular, it is his championing of our social – or HERD – nature that has impacted on practice in fields as disparate as political campaigning, the intelligence services and the green movement (as well, of course as marketing and behaviour change).

His previous books, *Welcome to the Creative Age* (Wiley 2003), *HERD* (Wiley 2007-9) and *I'll Have What She's Having* (with Profs Alex Bentley and

ABOUT THE AUTHOR

Mike O'Brien, MIT Press 2011) are both widely translated and discussed.

In a previous life, he held senior positions in creative businesses such as the revolutionary St Luke's Communications and the all-conquering Ogilvy Worldwide. He now works independently under the banner of HERD, in collaboration with a handful of partners.

Mark is a fellow of the Marketing Society and the Royal Society for the Promotion of Manufacturing and the Arts, an honorary Fellow of the Institute of Practitioners in Advertising and an active member of Creative Social.

He is based in London, but is mostly to be found at an airport near you. But on the whole, he'd rather be fishing.

ACKNOWLEDGEMENTS

It has now become a cliché – even in academic circles – for writers to praise all those who have commented or helped develop the ideas that follow. And then – bold as brass – to take sole responsibility for any errors that might be contained in the text. It often seems like false modesty.

This book is unusual in that it is about how the work of other hands can provide the tools for new and innovative solutions. And even this idea belongs to several other people – many but not all of whom are quoted in the text.

So the cliché holds and my modesty is real.

The intellectual finger prints of my key collaborators, Professor Alex Bentley and John V Willshire are all over this book – in different but equally important ways, they have shaped the ideas here directly. And John's Sharpie illustrations help bring some of the stories alive, I hope. Thank you both. Thanks also to Fraser Hamilton of Smithery and Tim Milne for sheepery, speech bubbles, cards and stickers.

Early readers like John, Gareth Kay, Liz Wilson, David Wood, Kevin Duncan and Julie Doleman have been incredibly useful in helping avoid embarrassing errors, as well as adding new or better examples and thoughts to the argument.

I've been struck by the kindness of the many strong supporters of the thinking as it has evolved and the suggestions they've made. This includes Gemma Greaves of the Marketing Society, Hugh 'gapingvoid' Macleod, Tom Fishburne, Lenny Murphy at Greenbook and Insight Innovation Exchange, Mark Brenner at MRS, Colin Grimshaw at Admap, John Kearon, Susan Griffin, Orlando Wood, Tom Ewing and Alex Batchelor at BrainJuicer, Geoff Grey, Paul Graham, Tom Daly, Alistair Barr, Giles Morrison and Ben Moore (both formerly of Sony Corporation), Dominic Grounsell, Sophie Rouse, Lee Payton, David Abraham, Mike O'Brien, Daniele Fiandaca, Elle Whitely and Mark Chalmers

ACKNOWLEDGEMENTS

at Creative Social, Morgwn Rimel and Cathy Haynes of the School of Life, Gareth Simpson, Alex Fleetwood (cofounder of the sadly now defunct Hide & Seek), Sue Unerman at MEC, Ramon Olle, Chris Clark, Graham Wood, Per Torberger, Eoin Pritchard, Richard Quance, Anthony Miller, Tim Hamill and Roger Goodchild of Schroder Investments, David Hieatt of Hiut Denim and the fabulous Do Lectures, Matthew Desmier of Silicon Beach, Joe Jenkins of Friends of the Earth, Stephen Maher and Nicole Yershon.

My team at Wiley – Jonathan Shipley and Jenny Ng – have also made the process of making the book a delight rather than a chore.

But most of all, it is my three favourite women who have made it possible to get this done: my sister Ros and her fabulous 140db musical box, my late mother Kath whose encouragement is still with me every day and my wonderful partner Sara who makes life so much better (and has no inhibitions about telling me when I'm waffling).

Best get on now. Things to do.

London, 2015

INDEX

42, significance of number 130–131

acetylsalicylic acid (ASA) 47
addiction 82
agenda translation strategy 118
alcoholic drinks market 75, 82, 110, 113, 123
Amazon 85
Amex 125
Anglo-Saxon culture 11
Apple
  customer capture 111
  developer community 117
  popularity strategies 73
  stores 24–25, 122
architecture 22–23, 49, 91–93
ASA (acetylsalicylic acid) 47
aspirin 47
Audi 105
Australia 12, 161, 165
'authority' strategies see 'expertise' strategies
autistic people 57
auto insurance 80
Avatar (film) 7
Avis 28, 104

babies, facial gestures 13
Bacardi 113, 117
Barrett, Michael 'Shaky' 3
Bass diffusions 140
Batchelor, Alex 143
Bateman, Matt 7
BE see behavioural economics
Beale Street 5

beer market 110, 113, 119
behaviour map 68–86
  alcoholic drinks market 75, 82
  car insurance 80
  charitable donations 79
  choice styles 71–73
  considered/rational choice 72
  data plotting 74
  deodorants market 81
  diffusion curves 74
  expert recommendation 73
  guesswork choice 72
  guided choice 73
  independent/social axis 69
  informed/uninformed axis 69
  insurance market 80
  peer-influenced choice 73
  politics 83
  popular music 78
  social choices 85
  voting 83
behavioural economics (BE) 70, 84–85, 110
Behavioural Insights Team, UK 146
benchmarking 25–26
'better mousetrap' strategy 102
'better' strategies 96, 100–107, 140–141, 152
Biden, Joe 9
biomimicry 47
bison hunting game 15
BMW 104, 105
Borg (Star Trek character) 11
boutique hotels 50
Bowie, David 35–36
Boyle, Susan 38, 78

brain function 57
Brainjuicer 48
brand names 24, 107
'broken society', riots and 158–159
buildings 22–23, 49, 91–93
'build to think' prototype, Pixar Studios 135
bullet train 47
Burroughs, William 36

Cable TV market 111
camera market 116
Cameron, David 156, 157, 158
Campbell, Joseph 8
Cancer Research UK 124
capital asset depreciation 143
Capitol building 92
cardiac surgery, lessons from Formula 1 pit team 172–175
car-hire business 28
car insurance 80
car market 104, 105, 106, 107
case studies 55
Catalonia 124
Catholic Church 53
'CeaseFire' programme 167
celebrity endorsement strategies 110, 125
celebrity magazines 94
Challenger Space Shuttle 36–37
challenges
  hand hygiene practices 148–152
  rioting 153–169
  social behaviour challenge 148–152
  strategy questioning 178–179
  tax return filing 142–147, 152

Chapter House (Motion) 35
charitable donations 79
cheating, perception of copying as 6–8
checklists 174–175
Chelsea Flower Show 94
China 22–25, 28
Chinese whispers game 32–33
choice styles *see* behaviour map
cholera 63–65
Christian traditions 53
cider market 123
clothing market 102, 107, 110
coffee shops 111
cognitive biases 56
Coke 102, 111, 113, 118, 119
collaboration with non-competitive brands
    strategy 113
comparative trial strategy 107
competitions and prizes strategy 112
computer games 15
confectionery market 105
conformism 10
considered/rational choice 72, 96, 100–107
Converse 104, 117
copying experts *see* 'expertise' strategies
copying peers choice *see* peer-influenced choice
Cova, Bernard 12
'cover artists' 4
Covey, Steven 54
Cowell, Simon 78
craftsmanship 36
creativity 39
Crimean War 66
Crufts Dog Show 118
Crumb, Robert 61
cultural behaviour, hand hygiene practices
    148–152
cultural identity strategy 117

cultural practice linking strategy 119
customer difficulty in leaving strategy 111
customer ease of choice strategy 110
customer loyalty rewards strategy 111
'cut-and-paste' writing 8
cutlery 16
'cut-up' technique 35–36

Damasio, Antonio 57
Danger Mouse (DJ) 44
Darwin, Charles 38
data, visualization of 63–67
deception, perception of copying as 6–8
'decision landscape' 70
de Mestral, Georges 46–47
deodorants market 81
department stores 119
Desigual 110
detergents market 103, 107
diffusion curves 74
diffusion of information 17–18
'discount machine' 15
discounts strategy 112, 145
Disney 7
Dove 118
dramatic advertising strategy 107
drawing 60–86
Dr Dre 125
'dubplate' 95
'Dude' persona exercise 51–52
Duggan, Mark 154
Dyson 102

egg market 106
eHi 28
Ekman, Paul 48
electronics market, consumer behaviour
    136–141

Eliot, TS 45
Elliott, Martin 172–175
Elvies festival 2–3
Elvis, history of name 3
Emergency Response Planning 37
emotional benefits strategy 104, 145
Energizer Bunny 107
energy market 111, 144
enthusiasm sharing strategy 122
epidemiological models 166
errors
    in reproduction/transmission 32–33, 37
    in surgery 175
Erwin, Kim 135
events strategy 112
evolution theory 38
exercises *see* games
expert endorsement strategies 116
'expertise' strategies 73, 97, 114–119,
        140–141, 147, 152
expert users strategies 116, 151

facial gestures, babies 13
fairy stories 53–54
fame-seeking strategy 110
fan gatherings strategy 124
fashion magazines 94
Father Ted (television programme) 44
Fern Gully (film) 7–8
films 7, 8, 116, 135
financial panics 124
financial penalties of delay strategy 113, 145
financial services 104, 110
finches, Darwin's 38
'fire-lighting' strategy 125
fishing equipment 106, 107
'fixing' broken things 40–43
folk stories 8, 53–54

food culture 16
forks 16
Formula 1 racing 172–175
forty-two, significance of number 130–131
Freddie Bell and the Bellboys 5
Frederick the Great 105
free product trial strategy 103
French Connection 110
French riots 161
fruit juice brand 102

Galaxy SOHO development 22
games
    Chinese whispers 32–33
    'Dude' persona 51–52
    'in-betweenies' 26–27
    'One Song to the Tune of Another' 44
    'Popular thing for a broken thing'
        42–43
gangs 164
'gapingvoid' (Hugh Macleod) 49
gardens 94–95
Gehry, Frank 49
Georgian pattern books 92
giveaways strategy 103
Google 118, 125
Great Ormond Street Hospital for Sick
    Children 172–175
green movement 118
Grey Album (Danger Mouse) 44
Guangdong province 23
guesswork choice 72, 96, 108–113
guided choice 73, 97, 114–119
guilds 36

Hadid, Zaha 22, 28
hand hygiene practices 148–152
Hardy of Alnwick 106, 107

hat-making 34
Heaney, Seamus 35
heart surgery 172–175
Heineken 110
Heinz 117, 122, 124
Hertz 28
hip-hop 95
Hoffman Process 116
hotels 50
Hound Dog (song) 4
human behaviour map see behaviour map
hunting of bison game 15

IBM 118
Ibn Khaldun 36
'I'll have what she's having' thinking
    style 14
illusionists 90
improv games 26–27
I'm Sorry I Haven't A Clue (radio
    programme) 44
'in-betweenies' game 26–27
individualism 10–12
inertia 144
infants, social learning 13
'influential' hypothesis, riots 164
information, social diffusion of 17–18
'information-deficit' communication model
    137
Innocent Drinks brand 118
innovation
    adoption time 19
    'fixing' broken things 40–43
    invention and 28–29, 180
    'leaving your job' exercise 52
    liminal nature of 50
insurance market 80, 111
intellectual property 6

internet 95
invention 28–29
Irn Bru 104
irrelevant/unusual features promotion
    strategy 113
Italy 12
Ives, Jonathan 6
Izzard, Eddie 70

Jarmusch, Jim 20
jeans 102
Jefferson, Thomas 91–92
John Lewis 106
journalism 8

Kahneman, Daniel 14, 70, 143
Kearon, John 48, 49
'Keep Calm' meme 30–31
Kia 106
'kinda' facility 57, 132
Kinnock, Neil 9
Kiva (connectedness and mutuality) 12
Kleon, Austin 62

La Casera 117
'lagom' 12
Laland, Kevin 15
Lansky, Bernard 5
LA Opera House 49
Latin cultures 12
La Via Catalana 124
'leaving your job' exercise 52
Lego 122
Lehrer, Jonah 8
Lenehan, John 90
Levi-Strauss 102
Lewis, CS 61
'listification' of success 54

literature
  see also stories
  creative copying 45
  'cut-up' technique 36
  map-making 60–61
  translations 35
littleBits 116
London
  cholera outbreak map 63–65
  Olympics Games 6
  riots 153–159, 160
Lubetkin, Berthold 93
luxury brands 103

Macleod, Hugh 49
magazines 94
Magic Circle 90
Magners 123
Makey Makey 122
manufacturing industry 23–25, 137
map-making 60–86
  behaviour map 68–86
  polar area diagrams 66, 67
  Soho cholera outbreak map 63–65
market research 48
Mars brands 105, 118
Martin, George RR 29
'mash-up' culture 44–45
Matisse, Henri 34
McKinsey 26
media, riots and 165
medicine
  see also surgery
  outcomes 143
  visualization of data 63–67
Meltzoff, Andrew 13
membership recruitment strategy 125
memes 18, 30–31

Mesoudi, Alex 15
Metroland 93
millinery 34
mobile phones 24
'mock Tudor' style 92–93
Monroe, Ohio 17
Moore, Henry 58
Moore, Scotty 5
Moran, Matthew 162
Motion, Andrew 35
Motorola 52
movies 7, 8, 116, 135
Multiples: 12 Stories in 18 Languages by 61
  authors 35
music
  'cover artists' 4
  'cut-up' technique 35–36
  hip-hop 95
  'mash-up' technique 44
  streaming of 70
'my favourite club' trap 132–133
mygizmo challenge 136–141, 152

NASA 36
National Trust 94
Nescafe 112
Newcomen, Thomas 40
'new dimension of better' strategy 105
news, diffusion of information 17–18
News International 112
'new test of better' strategy 103
Nightingale, Florence 66–67
Nikon 116
novel ideas 19
'nudgers' 84–85

O'Brien, Michael 15
Olympic Games, London 6

'One Song to the Tune of Another' game 44
organized approach 55–56
original and best strategy 102
originality 19, 29, 180
over-engineering strategy 107

packaging strategies 119, 151
Palladio, Andrea 91
pattern books 90–127, 179
  architecture 91–93
  'better' strategies 96, 100–107
  'expertise' strategies 114–119
  gardens 94–95
  how to use strategies 98
  internet 95
  Magic Circle 90
  music 95
  'popularity' strategies 120–125
  'salience' strategies 108–113
Pearson, Geoffrey 160
peer-influenced choice 73, 97, 120–125
penalties of delay strategy 113
Pepsi 102, 107, 119
performance 39
Peter the Great 45–46
pharmaceutical industry 47
Phillips, Peter 2
Phillips, Sam 125
Picasso 45
Pinker, Steven 61
Pixar Studios 135
plagiarism 8
Pocahontas (film) 7
poetry 35, 45
polar area diagrams 66, 67
police 154, 169
politics 6, 9, 83
Polycell 103

pop-art 32
popular choice strategy 122
popular music 78
'Popular thing for a broken thing' game 42–43
'popularity' strategies 97, 120–125, 147
potatoes 105, 117
Presley, Elvis 2–5
pricing strategies 103, 106, 112
prizes strategy 112
procurement contracts 43

quantification strategy 105
'Quattro Libri' (Palladio) 91
questions vs. answers 131

rational choice 72, 96, 100–107
Red Stripe brand 119
religions 53
reproduction/transmission errors 32–33, 37
'resetting the default' strategy 110
restriction of supply strategy 105
rewards for customer loyalty strategy 111
'rinse and repeat' exercise 49
rioting 153–169
    'broken society' causation 158–159
    causes of 158–159, 162–163
    historical perspective 160
    'influential' hypothesis 164
    listening to the rioters 159
    London riots 153–159
    media role 165
    police response 169
    punishment of rioters 169
    societal collapse causation 158–159
    spontaneous nature of 164–165
    stopping spread of 168–169
    violence transmission 166–167

ritual behaviour around brand strategy 124
Royal Horticultural Society 94
Russia 45–46

Sacks, Jonathan 153
'salience' strategies 96, 108–113
sampling, music 95
'sanitize', cultural associations 149
satisfaction guaranteed strategy 106
scarcity of product strategy 105
Schumpeter, Joseph 29
Schweppes 106
sculptures 17, 34
secrecy 90
self-help books 54
Sennett, Richard 36, 62
Serpentine Gallery 22
Shaking Stevens 3
Shanzai products 24–25, 28
shared cultural identity strategy 117
sharing enthusiasm for product strategy 122
Shraeger, Ian 50
Sierra Club 118
Single White Copying 25–26
'singularity' trap 133
Slutkin, Gary 166, 167
smartphones 24
Smith, Justin 34
smoking 110
Snow, John 63–65
Snow White (folk story) 8
social acceptability strategy 123, 146
social behaviour, hand hygiene practices 148–152
social choices 85
social identity strategy 119, 151
social learning 13, 15–16
social media 17–18, 165, 168

social networks 82
social structures strategy 117
soft drinks market 102, 104, 111, 113, 117, 118, 119
software market 110
Soho, cholera outbreak map 63–65
Solid Rock Church, Monroe, Ohio 17
'something to believe' in strategy 118
Sony 107, 116
Southern Africa 11
Space Shuttle 36–37
Spain 110, 112
spear design, computer game 15
sports events 124
sport utility vehicles (SUVs) 107
Starmer, Keir 169
Star Wars (film series) 8
steam engines 40
Stepney, Nigel 174
Stevenson, Robert Louis 60–61
stories 7–8, 60–61
    see also literature
strategies
    see also pattern books
    choosing 134
    copying well 134–135
    hand hygiene challenge 148–152
    'my favourite club' trap 132–133
    mygizmo challenge 136–141
    new model 176–179
    questioning of 178–179
    rioting 153–169
    'singularity' trap 133
    tax returns challenge 142–147, 152
    traps for strategists 132–133
street gangs 164
students 8
suburban architecture 92–93

INDEX

success 'listification' 54
Sundance Film Festival 116
Sun Records 125
superiority of product strategy 106
supply restriction strategy 105
surgery
    see also medicine
    error counts 175
    lessons from Formula 1 pit team
        172–175
surprise strategy 104
SUVs (sport utility vehicles) 107
Sweden 12
Sydney riots 161, 165
System 1 and 2 thinking 14, 143

tax return filing 142–147, 152
Telco industry 26
telephone companies 111
television market 72, 111
'terroir' 106
Thames Town, China 23
theatre 39
theft, perception of copying as 6–8
thinking, types of 14, 143
Thornton, Willie Mae 'Big Mama' 4
Tianjin 23

togetherness strategies 118, 124
Tolkien, JRR 61
tonic water market 106
'Touchdown Jesus' statue 17
trains 47
translations 35
transport 47
traps for strategists 132–133
Treasure Island (Stevenson) 60–61
TripAdvisor 85
Tropicana fruit juice 102
Tutu, Desmond 11
Twitter 17–18

ubiquity strategy 111
Ubuntu (connectedness and mutuality) 11–12
Unilever 111
United Kingdom (UK)
    Behavioural Insights Team 146
    energy companies 111
    tax authority 123
United States (US)
    'CeaseFire' programme 167
    LA Opera House 49
    violence 'epidemics' 166
unusual/irrelevant features promotion
        strategy 113

Velcro 47
'velvet rope' strategy 105
violence, transmission of 166–167
    see also rioting
visible choices strategies 123
vodka 82
Volkswagen 106
voting 83

Warhol, Andy 32
Watt, James 40–41
'we' cultures 11–12
WEIRD (Western, educated,
    industrialized, rich and democratic)
    societies 11
'what kinda?' questions 132
Wilde, Oscar 10
Willshire, John V. 42, 62
wine market 106
'wisdom of crowds' phenomenon 48
word-of-mouth marketers 85
Worsley, Henry 161

*Index compiled by Indexing Specialists (UK)
    Ltd*

NOTES